BRITI
BEC...... ..LLIZL

A Peace Corps Memoir
1971-1973

First Printing
July 2014

No. 1205 of 1500

Ted W. Cox

Library of Congress Cataloguing-in-Publication
Data
Cox, Ted W., 1947-
When British Honduras Became Belize—
A Peace Corps Memoir, 1971-1973

Includes index
ISBN 978-0-9760891-4-8

The following credit must accompany any photo
taken from this book (except photos attributed to
third parties):
    Text and image courtesy of Ted W. Cox

Although this book is written in good faith,
mistakes are inevitable. The author recognizes any
error that appears in the narrative as his own.
Users are encouraged to take precautions and do
their own research before relying on information
provided herein.

1. Peace Corps. 2. British Honduras. 3. Belize.
4. Sierra Leone. I. Title.

July 2014
Cover art: Envelope collage from USA, Sierra Leone
and Belize by Zac Bunsen

Old World Deli Publications
Corvallis, Oregon, U.S.A.
www.oldworlddelipublications.com

Printed in the United States of America
United Graphics, LLC
Mattoon, Illinois

ii

DEDICATION

To the People of Belize, for
whom I have the deepest respect,
and to my loving wife, Veronica.

Map A: Central American nations

Map B. Districts of Belize

Map C. Major cities and towns of Belize

CONTENTS

ACKNOWLEDGEMENTS   ix
LIST OF PICTURES   xi
LIST OF MAPS   xix
FOREWORD by Rob Thurston   xxi
PREFACE   xxv
PRESS RELEASE   xxvii

1. Introduction
   California to West Africa   1
2. Welcome to British Honduras   31
3. A Stormy Start   43
4. Belize City Life   49
5. Belmopan   75
6. Getting to Work   85
7. Garifuna Settlement Days, 1971   95
8. National Track and Field Course   103
9. Equipment, Athletes, and Preparation   113
10. Regional and National Track and Field
    Competitions, 1972   131
11. Danger from the Border   143
12. Governor Sir Richard Posnett   151
13. On War and Peace   157
14. Isolated in Punta Gorda   169
15. Glimpses of Peace Corps Life   175
16. Girlfriends
    Baron Bliss   197
17. The Cayo District   211
18. Yo Creek, Inter-Primary School Field
    Day   219
19. Triangular Track and Field Meet, 1972   227
20. Heading for the States   239
21. The Fairweathers
    Arrival of Devon and Dorset Regiment   249
22. Physical Performance Testing   257

23. Peace Corps Midterm Conference 275
24. National Agricultural Show, Belmopan
    Developmental Competition, Belize City 281
25. Garifuna Settlement Days, 1972 289
26. United Nations
    Christmas 1972 307
27. A Garifuna Farm 317
28. Testing in Punta Gorda
    Return to Belize City 333
29. To San Pedro for Testing and Fun 341
30. Regional and National Track and Field
    Competitions, 1973 351
31. Stann Creek and San Ignacio
    Inter-Primary School Field Days 367
32. Triangular Track and Field Meet, 1973 381
33. Hosting the Rowdy Texans 393
34. When British Honduras Became Belize
    My Farewell 397
35. Epilogue 403

PROGRESS REPORT 417
INDEX 425
CREATIVE COMMONS ATTRIBUTIONS 441
ABOUT THE AUTHOR 442
ALSO BY TED W. COX 443

ACKNOWLEDGEMENTS

From the time this project got underway, I have been fortunate to have a series of talented friends and acquaintances involved to make this book possible:

Rob Thurston	Corvallis, Oregon
David S. Luft	Corvallis, Oregon
Zac Bunsen	Corvallis, Oregon
Greg Dinkens	Corvallis, Oregon
John W. Nott	Corvallis, Oregon
Grace Foster	Corvallis, Oregon
Pat Mooney	Corvallis, Oregon
Jessica L. Mortimer	Corvallis, Oregon
Victor F. Price	Corvallis, Oregon
David Anderson	Austin, Texas
Consuelo (Cheli) Z. Anderson	Austin, Texas
Neal Hammond	Phoenix, Arizona
Rick and Ysela Sharp	California
Fred Evans	Ladyville, Belize
Randolph Johnson	Belize City, Belize
Adrian Roe	Belize City, Belize
Mary Jane Robb	Fowlerville, Michigan
John Russell	Corvallis, Oregon
Sistie Harmes (Fairweather)	Ladyville, Belize
Darius Martinez	Belmopan, Belize
Tarmo Jaagus	Strawberry, California
Marilyn Hileman	Pasadena, California
Janet L. O'Day	Lebanon, Oregon
Shirley Brennan	Corvallis, Oregon
Mark Williams	Upland, California
Leni Jo Usher	Belize City, Belize
Jane White	Corvallis, Oregon
Harland Pratt	Corvallis, Oregon
Rudy Gentle	N. Plainsfield, NJ
Carole Baldwin	San Diego, California

LIST OF PICTURES

1. Taiama, Sierra Leone   4
2. Bo Teacher Training College (BTTC)   7
3. Physical education class   8
4. Neighbor children   9
5. Bamboo playground   10
6. Track and field clinic   11
7. Christmas celebration   13
8. Ramadan celebration   14
9. Geographical club trip, Bonthe   20
10. Driving lane changeover   20
11. Four friends   21
12. Cheerful beggars   21
13. Boxing Day   22
14. Rugby champions, Marampa Mines   23
15. Coronation Field   24
16. Coronation Field   25
17. BTTC Torwama Campus   26
18. Peace Corps Director Alex Frankson,
    British Honduras   32
19. Associate PC Director Kelly Compton   32
20. Office Administrator Barbara Harris   33
21. Associate PC Director Rob Thurston   33
22. Xunantunich   36
23. Minister of Local Government   38
24. Introduction letter   39
25. Minister of Education   40
26. Entrance to Haulover Creek   50
27. Victoria Street, Belize City   51
28. Craig Street, 1975   51
29. Four friends   52
30. East Canal Street, 1915   53
31. Eve Street Canal, 1975   54
32. Swing Bridge   56
33. Public Market   57

34. Haulover Creek   57
35. Masonic burial procession   58
36. Government Customs Building   60
37. Shanty shops, 1975   62
38. Drying laundry, 1975   63
39. National Stadium   64
40. G. Hinkson and B. Lightburn, 1975   67
41. Four friends   68
42. The Rose Garden   69
43. Bob Moriano in Ladyville   71
44. Belmopan ready for settlement, 1970   76
45. Old-growth mahogany tree   78
46. Social Development Department   79
47. George Price home, Belmopan   80
48. 50-mph speed limit sign, Belmopan   82
49. First day on the job, Belize City   85
50. New Ministry Offices   86
51. Walter Bennett   88
52. PCV Kroehl and Jones   91
53. PCV Neil Policelli   92
54. Alexandrina Martinez   97
55. Tropical Storm Laura   97
56. Peace Corps couple   99
57. Martinez family from tower   99
58. Alexandrina Martinez and sisters   100
59. Track course outline   104
60. Track course certificate   105
61. Track course, MCC Grounds   106
62. Track course participants   107
63. Dudley Augustine, Orange Walk   108
64. Junior Secondary #2 woodshop   113
65. Transferring sand to shore   114
66. Track course, Corozal   115
67. Eastern track meet   115
68. Track course, laying out lanes   117
69. Percy Eagan   117
70. Constructing a wet marking box   118

71. Constructing a wet marking box 118
72. Constructing a wet marking box 118
73. PCV Chris Dixon 119
74. Ned Pitts 119
75. Dorla Flowers, Eastern track meet 121
76. James Usher and Dick Slater 127
77. Secondary school track program 131
78. High jump 133
79. 100-meter race 133
80. Distance race 134
81. Southern track meet program 135
82. BHAAA president's message 136
83. Officials, National track meet 140
84. Girls' race, National track meet 140
85. Wesley College wins 141
86. Squaring mahogany, 1920s 145
87. Woodcutter, 1920s 146
88. Devon and Dorset demonstration 149
89. Governor at Queen's Parade, c.1973 153
90. Dignitaries with Prince Philip, 1975 154
91. Blue Creek, north British Honduras 158
92. Camp Holdfast 163
93. Cadenas Observation Post 163
94. Cayo Observation Post 164
95. Salamanca Camp 164
96. Southern Highway bridge 169
97. Southern Highway bridge swamped 170
98. Fairview Elementary, Punta Gorda 173
99. Neal Hammond, Bevis Ranch 180
100. Fitting chicken feed mixer 182
101. PCV Barbara MacLeod 185
102. Petroglyph Cave, rappelling 187
103. Explorers, Petroglyph Cave entrance 188
104. Don Warren and PCVs, Dos Bocas 190
105. Near La Unión, Mexico 190
106. PVC Rick Sharp cutting bamboo 192
107. Bamboo for Belize Teachers' College 193

108. College students constructing tower   194
109. Author supervising construction   194
110. Construction nears completion   195
111. College volleyball game   195
112. Bliss Institute, 1975   198
113. Leni Jo Usher and the author   199
114. Robert Mitchell   201
115. Sistie Fairweather and friends   203
116. Sistie's Dance Troupe   204
117. Shaun Stewart, Bliss Institute   205
118. Solie Arquellas, Bliss Institute   206
119. Baron Bliss River Regatta   207
120. Competitors finish race   207
121. Baron Bliss River Regatta   208
122. Play director Frank Cervantes   208
123. A scene from *Bamboo Clump*   209
124. Hawkesworth Bridge, Cayo   211
125. Field marking, San Ignacio   213
126. Preparing the field   214
127. Telephone exchange   214
128. District officer's house   216
129. Field day, San Ignacio   217
130. Volunteers visit Yo Creek   220
131. Inter-Primary School Field Day   221
132. Starter PCV Neil Policelli, Yo Creek   221
133. Relay race   222
134. Long jump   222
135. Long jump   223
136. Recording scores   223
137. James Usher   224
138. Boyfriends   224
139. Girlfriends   225
140. Cox, Carcano and Hinkson   227
141. Officials plan triangular meet   228
142. BH Volunteer Guard Band   229
143. Presenting the team flags   230
144. Distance race, Triangular meet   231

145. Relaying results at the finish line 232
146. The finish line 232
147. Steve Perera receives an award 233
148. Medley race award presentation 233
149. BHAAA javelin throw 234
150. Grenadier Guard pole vaults 234
151. Fosbury Flop high jump 235
152. BHAAA shot put 235
153. Grenadier Guard tug of war 236
154. Cox family, San Diego 241
155. Cox family, San Diego 242
156. Smithford Products sign 243
157. Smithford Products worker 244
158. Corozal waterfront 247
159. Lt. Colonel D.N.A. Fairweather 250
160. Barbara Harris and children 251
161. Rugby at Airport Camp 252
162. PCV Rick Sharp, line out 255
163. Cover: fitness booklet 259
164. Solomon Constanza in tower 261
165. Orange Walk from tower 262
166. Pull-up, Belize Technical College 264
167. Sit-up, Jr. Secondary #2 265
168. Shuttle run, Austin High School 265
169. Broad jump, St. John's College 266
170. 50-yard dash, Muffles College 266
171. Softball throw, Western High School 267
172. Run-walk, Belmopan Comprehensive 267
173. Letter from CEO Dave Leacock 272
174. PCV Midterm Conference 276
175. Impromptu jam 276
176. PCVs on the reef 278
177. Robert Mitchell 282
178. National Agricultural Show 283
179. Battalion demonstration 283
180. Rodeo 284
181. Bill Lightburn, Development meet 285

182. Kolberg and Hinkson marking track 286
183. Cyclists 286
184. Official Gilmore Hinkson 287
185. Darius Martinez and children 289
186. Gaynor Martinez, Stann Creek 290
187. Flowers children 291
188. North Stann Creek bridge 291
189. Alexandrina Martinez 292
190. Children, Stann Creek 293
191. Celebrating at Golden Bowl 294
192. Relaxing at Kennedy Club 294
193. John Canoe 295
194. Miss Belmopan 1972 296
195. Stann Creek River 297
196. Settlement Days Reenactment 298
197. Paddling upriver 298
198. Settlers arrive 299
199. Unloading a boat 299
200. Welcoming a traveler 300
201. Jerris Valentine helping unload 301
202. Getting off the boat 302
203. Walking to church 303
204. Welcoming travelers 303
205. Music in the streets 304
206. Drumming to church 305
207. Vin Lawrence, Belize City 309
208. Horse races, National Stadium 314
209. Nearing the finish line 314
210. Ann Noralez, Stann Creek 318
211. Domingo Martinez 319
212. Government Rest House 321
213. Stann Creek from tower 321
214. Martinez farm 323
215. Cassava bread 324
216. Grating cassava 326
217. Squeezing wowla 327
218. Squeezing starch 329

219. Extracting starch 330
220. Carib women planting cassava 331
221. Stann Creek Airport 334
222. Francis Hecker, Punta Gorda 335
223. Roy Bradley, Belmopan 337
224. Cycle race, National Stadium 337
225. Bill Lightburn 338
226. Louis Sylvestre 339
227. *Emma* docked at San Pedro 342
228. Mangrove swamp 343
229. Enrique Staines and a barracuda 345
230. Softball, St. Peter's College 346
231. Hunting at San Pedro 348
232. Sister Leona, Muffles College 352
233. Judges stand, Orange Walk 353
234. Northern Divisional Track Meet 353
235. Honored guests 354
236. Officiating at the meet 355
237. Relay hand-off 356
238. Perfect hand-off 356
239. High jump 357
240. Distance run 357
241. Completing the distance run 358
242. Overall champion Fletcher College 358
243. Accepting the award 359
244. Start of the 100-meter race 361
245. 100-meter sprint 362
246. Distance run 362
247. Albert Lovell to the rescue 363
248. Ned Pitts marks field, Stann Creek 364
249. Hernan Ochaeta, San Ignacio 368
250. Hernan Ochaeta places lane marker 369
251. Marking lanes, Stann Creek 370
252. Laying sand 371
253. Inter-Primary School Field Day 372
254. At the finish line 372
255. Accepting an award 373

256. Norrin O. Meighan, San Ignacio   375
257. San Ignacio ribbons   376
258. Inter-Primary School Field Day   376
259. Egg balance   377
260. Record keepers   378
261. Relay hand-off   378
262. Teamwork   379
263. Signing into competition   379
264. Ready for the sprint   379
265. Triangular Track and Field Meet   381
266. Sgt. Bill Hodgson, Belize City   382
267. Opening ceremonies   383
268. Javelin throw   384
269. High jump   384
270. Irish Guard competitor   385
271. Bruce Bowing throwing discus   385
272. Shot put   386
273. Eric Waight   387
274. Chadwich Usher in medley   388
275. Albert Lovell, tug of war   389
276. Volunteer Guard team   389
277. Irish Guard, tug of war   390
278. Ted of Rob of Ted   390
279. Belize Rugby Club   396
280. Airport Camp rugby game   399
281. Soldiers relaxing, Airport Camp   400
282. Rivero at the airport   401
283. Rick Sharp officiates   406
284. Francisco Cervantes, Victoria Street   408
285. Bill Lightburn, Euphrates Ave.   410
286. Bill's granddaughter Maureen   412
287. Informal deed   413

LIST OF MAPS

A. Central American nations   iv
B. Districts of Belize   v
C. Major cities and towns
    of Belize   vi
D. Sierra Leone, West Africa   3
E. Selected locations in Belize   143
F. Military map of Belize, 1975   160

FOREWORD

"Hey, Ted mon, how keeping?" With those words, I reconnected with Ted W. Cox in Corvallis, Oregon in 1993 after a span of over 20 years since we'd last seen each other in Belize. Back in 1972 Ted was serving there as a Peace Corps Volunteer (PCV) charged with developing the aspiring nation's track and field program.

I had the good fortune of being one of two Peace Corps supervisory staff and got to know Ted, and the other sixty-some PCVs there. Ted easily stood out from the others, having previously served for two years in Sierra Leone teaching health, physical education and coaching at a teacher's college. He brought an air of professionalism and confidence, not to mention cross-cultural and, to an astonishing degree, language skills, which most of his recently graduated PCV cohorts hadn't yet attained. He was reputed to be the only PCV in Belize who got off the plane already understanding and speaking what passed for the Caribbean Creole spoken in Belize. That was due, I'm told, to a common African mother-tongue structure, layered over by colonial English. This was widely spoken across Anglophone West Africa and transported by slaves brought by the British to the West

Indies and Belize. This language base, coupled with his social nature and affability, made Ted an instant hit with both Belizeans and compatriots alike.

Who better then, to tell the story of building a nationally unifying track and field program precisely as British Honduras moved forward on the path to an independent Belize?

As Ted relates, his was a people-to-people exercise uniting schools, towns, districts, government, civil society and, in what may seem odd, the British army. In effect, it was an exercise that reinforced the fundamental cooperation required in successful nation building.

Ted is much too modest to say so, but his Peace Corps role was truly Herculean—establishing national physical education benchmark data, training track and field coaches and officials, improvising basic tracks and facilities in far-flung villages and towns, and bringing qualified athletes to national arenas—and all of this against a backdrop of seasonal hurricanes and threats of armed invasion from neighboring (but decidedly un-neighborly) Guatemala. Ironically, those threats also provided Ted with an important source of human and material support through the British army presence.

Ted's account draws upon his journals and many letters written to his mother, Florence Cox. These reveal a caring son, and also speak to many aspects of his work and personal life. He shares stories and incidents, some of which might make a mother wince. Teddy, as he is known within the family circle, was a partying man. His social skills and true interest in people created friendships and rapport that underlay his remarkable success. Ted was also an avid photographer, making space in his cramped quarters for a darkroom. He shares many images of the early days of track and field, Peace Corps life, and historical moments in Belize.

As Peace Corps Volunteers around the world will testify, it is the personal connections that ultimately matter. Ted is no exception, but would add that timing put him in the right place at the right time. Maybe so, but he was the right man for the job and he did it "only too good, mon"!

PREFACE

A few years ago I received a bundle of letters from my sister in California. I had mailed them one by one to my mother over thirty years earlier from West Africa and Central America while serving as a Peace Corps Volunteer. Three years ago this correspondence, coupled with journals and personal pictures, became the starting point of the following story.

I think that in today's world, stories like this will be lost because of deleted files as the information age moves paperless through our lives. But then again, if I had not decided to move on this project now, old age and forgetfulness would have fated my paper trail to an actual trashcan and the story forgotten.

After forty years, memories fade and one can easily embellish past events as larger than life. Wishing to avoid exaggerations and minimize errors, I have written as best I know by using interviews, research, pictures, journals, letters and attentive editors.

I hope you enjoy taking this journey to a previous time in living memory.

Ted W. Cox
February 1, 2014

PRESS RELEASE

In July 1971, President Richard Nixon issued an executive order that folded the Peace Corps with several domestic service programs into a new Federal Volunteer service agency called ACTION.

In 1981 the Peace Corps again became an independent Federal Agency, no longer a part of ACTION.

The following article regarding the author was distributed by ACTION for immediate press release in May 1973.

ACTION NEWS

PEACE CORPS • VISTA • UNIVERSITY YEAR FOR ACTION
FOSTER GRANDPARENT PROGRAM • RETIRED SENIOR VOLUNTEER PROGRAM
SERVICE CORPS OF RETIRED EXECUTIVES • ACTIVE CORPS OF EXECUTIVES

Office of Public Affairs, 806 Connecticut Ave., N.W., Washington, D.C. 20525

FOR IMMEDIATE RELEASE   CONTACT: NISSEN DAVIS
                                                   (202) 382-1911

Peace Corps Volunteer:

ONTARIO MAN POPULARIZES TRACK
AND FIELD IN BRITISH HONDURAS

BELIZE CITY, British Honduras -- Track and field competition
in British Honduras is growing by leaps and bounds, thanks largely
to the efforts of Ted Cox, a Peace Corps volunteer from Ontario,
Calif.

Cox, a graduate of Chaffey College, Alta Loma, Calif.
and nearby La Verne College, is now British Honduras National Track
and Field Director.

As large as Massachusetts, but with a population of only 122,000,
British Honduras is sandwiched between Mexico and Guatemala, facing
the Caribbean. Belize, as it will soon be officially called, has
been home to Cox since 1971.

Before that he was a Peace Corps volunteer in Sierra Leone, West
Africa, where he taught physical education and athletics at a teachers
training college, organized field days and boxing tournaments
throughout the country, and helped the National Sports Council
organize clinics for coaches.

Following two years in Africa, Ted volunteered to extend his service in the Peace Corps and in August of 1971 reported to the British Honduras Ministry of Local Government as National Track and Field Director. His job: to get track and field firmly set in this Central American British colony.

Ted trains athletes for possible international competition sets up regular athletic programs in secondary schools and clubs and has inaugurated a national record-keeping system. He has written a 50-page illustrated book entitled National Track and Field Course - British Honduras Amateur Athletic Association which enables coaches to conduct a nine-session course on athletic rules and coaching techniques.

"I wrote the book because the country can't afford a paid, full time track and field director. Now the coaches should be able to manage quite well after I am gone," he said.

During his two years in British Honduras, Ted has trained dozens of volunteer athletic coaches throughout the country, including teachers, policemen and district officers. Thanks to his efforts British Honduras held its first National Inter Secondary School Meet in April, 1972 - and a second and larger event in April, 1973.

Since last October Ted has been conducting physical performance testing, as conducted by the American Association for Health, Physical

-more-

Education and Recreation. He has tested more than 1,000 9th and 10th grade boys and has established norms for British Honduras.

A native of Eugene, Ore., Ted is the son of Mrs. Florence Cox of 921 Jasmine St., Ontario, Calif. He graduated from Montclair High School, Montclair, Calif. in 1965, obtained an Associate in Arts degree from Chaffey Jr. College, Alta Loma, Calif. in 1967, and a BA in Physical Education from La Verne College, La Verne, Calif. in 1969.

Ted Cox is one of 129 Peace Corps volunteers engaged in physical education and recreation programs around the world, and is one of 48 volunteers serving in British Honduras in education, health, agriculture, vocational education and specialized programs.

The Peace Corps, with about 7000 volunteers in 59 developing countries, is part of ACTION, the citizens service corps established by President Nixon in July, 1971 to administer federal volunteer programs at home and overseas. Michael P. Balzano, Jr. is director-designate of ACTION.

ACTION's domestic programs are Volunteers in Service to America (VISTA), Foster Grandparent Program, Service Corps of Retired Executives (SCORE), Active Corps of Executives (ACE), Retired Senior Volunteer Program (RSVP) and University Year for ACTION (UYA).

XXX

1
Introduction
California to West Africa

The judge was not happy with my request at traffic court in Pomona, California. I had just pleaded guilty to running a red light. The year was 1969 and the fine $10. At the time I was a senior attending college in the nearby town of LaVerne. With the courtroom full of individuals waiting their turn, I spoke up and said something like, "Excuse me, Your Honor, but I am a college student without a job. Is there an alternative to paying this fine?" He answered coolly, "You can spend the weekend at the Los Angeles County Jail." Without hesitation, my reply was "O.K." The courtroom broke out in laughter. The judge was not humored though. He granted the request and sent me on my way. While leaving the room I asked the clerk what time I should report to jail. He ignored the question and told me to move on.

I soon experienced why serving time should be avoided. On the scheduled day, my college roommate drove me to the jail in downtown Los Angeles. I spent Saturday and Sunday with a number of other weekenders, men who had jobs during the week while serving sentences on weekends.

Years later I discovered that during the 1970s, the Los Angeles County Jail became a dangerous place to be imprisoned. But in 1969, there were other hazards lurking. For instance, inmates received chest x-rays each time they checked into the system. DDT, which was banned in 1972, was also administered during check-in to kill parasites. The guards gave the dusting to the armpits and private areas. This happened to all of us.

Can you imagine! Some of these guys were serving over a dozen consecutive weekends and went through the same check-in procedure every time!

I was twenty-two years old and didn't consider going to jail to be reckless, but rather a journey to experience and understand incarceration.

The previous fall, a Peace Corps recruiter visited the La Verne campus and talked about becoming a volunteer. This adventure sounded so good that I decided to submit an application. Within weeks an invitation came to train in Sierra Leone, West Africa. I was about to learn first hand what a great institution the United States Peace Corps was.

D. Sierra Leone, West Africa.

Soon after being accepted, I heard that a young man from Sierra Leone lived nearby. I had the good fortune to meet Sigismond Thomas, who was a student living in Ontario. He became my introduction to African culture. During our first meeting he taught me how to say in Krio (Creole): "Hi friend. How are you?" – "Padi kusheh-o. Aw di bodi?" and "I give thanks to God" – "Ah tell God tanki."

Months later, I became friends with his parents who lived in Taiama, Sierra Leone, a small village located on the southern highway to Freetown.

1. *Taiama, Sierra Leone. Mr. and Mrs. Thomas in their back yard. They survived a deadly cholera epidemic in 1970-71 that swept throughout the country. Sixty people died in Taiama during the outbreak. 1971.*

Graduation day at La Verne College was June 15, 1969. Five days later, I was on a flight to Philadelphia for Peace Corps staging, a process that involved physical exams, health vaccinations, and general Peace Corps indoctrination. There were hundreds of trainees present at staging. All were invited to serve in various countries around Africa.

After a week in Philadelphia, 180 of us left for Sierra Leone and in-country training. We received intensive language study, area studies, and experienced a local family home stay. Seventy of us stayed in Freetown for seven weeks, teaching tenth grade general science at one of Freetown's premier secondary schools, Albert Academy. With the end of our teaching experience, we were sworn in.

Following the ceremonies, Sierra Leone Peace Corps Director Joe Kennedy (no relation to JFK), inquired about my degree in physical education and invited me to be one of six volunteers to be located at various teacher training colleges throughout the country. I think that I was the only jock in the group and was delighted to accept.

Letter Home
August 16, 1969
Sierra Leone

I've finished Peace Corps Training summer school at Albert Academy in Freetown and found out some very flattering news. There are six openings at teacher training colleges around the country. This is a prized and highly desired job in the program. Teacher training colleges prepare students to be teachers, who in turn will teach their students. Of the 70 Peace Corps trainees in education, I was one of six chosen for this job. And get this, I'll be teaching physical education, coaching and a subject like anatomy or health. I can hardly believe it. I think the six of us will move out of Freetown a week early to observe primary schools upcountry.

My placement was at Bo Teacher Training College located in Bo Town, a city of about 30,000 people. There I taught classes in health and physical education, and coached and supervised student practicums at elementary schools.

2. *Bo Town. Bo Teacher Training College (BTTC). Faculty and janitor at Kulanda Town Campus. Peace Corps Volunteer (PCV) Ted W. Cox at bottom right, PCV Frank Fletcher, third from left, principal of the college, Mr. Mathews (from India), bottom left. 1969.*

3. Bo Town. BTTC student conducting a physical education class during a practicum at a primary school. 1970.

4. Bo Town. Many of these neighbor children were related to the author's landlady, Mrs. Tucker. 1969.

5. *Bo Town. The author supervised the building of bamboo playground equipment at various elementary schools throughout Bo. Above, the principal of the Seventh Day Adventist Primary School is testing a new swing. March 1970.*

6. *Bo Town. Participants in a track and field clinic sponsored by the National Sports Council. The author, top row, second from left, PCV Bob Petterson, top row fourth from left. Conductors of the course from Freetown were Assistant Director of Sports, I.E. Benjamin, top row second from right, and N.K. Nicol, top row far right. November 1970.*

In December 1969, I decided to celebrate Christmas with a Sierra Leone feel. I had already seen Ken Jackson, an Englishman, dressed as Santa Claus and being pulled in a cart. He was tossing candy to people while bellowing "Ho Ho Ho" and "Merry Christmas." In my scheme, I planned to wear a traditional costume and dance for children's amusement while handing out small presents and candy on Christmas

11

Day. Instead of seeking money for my efforts, as was the custom with traditional 'fun' dancers, I would give in the spirit of Christmas.

Over 400 balloons containing candy and trinkets were taped to a tree stem which I shook as I danced through the neighborhood. (See YouTube video, "Sierra Leone Peace Corps Christmas in Bo, 1969.") For about forty-five minutes we were having fun, as dozens of children eventually emerged into the street. Despite my being covered from head to toe in my costume, the children were not fooled about my identity. After the first thirty minutes they started chanting, "Pumwai na debul, hay hay." We all danced to the rhythm they sang. *Pumwai* is the word for white man in the Mende language. *Na debul* is Krio language for "is a devil".[1] The children were chanting, "White man is a devil."

The following year I went into the streets again. But this time, instead of Christmas, I chose to observe the end of Ramadan, as many Muslims live in Bo. Ramadan is a special month of the year for Muslims worldwide. This is the time of fasting, observed during the ninth month of the Islamic calendar, so dates change from year to year. The day after Ramadan ends, children traditionally receive gifts and candy from adults as tokens of love and goodwill.

12

With this in mind, I again danced in a traditional tribal costume, giving away mostly candy, some money and a few small presents. After these holidays I was sometimes addressed in the street by children as "Pumwai na debul".

Ted W. Cox

7. *Bo Town. The author preparing to celebrate Christmas in the streets with children. December 1969.*

8. Bo Town. End of Ramadan celebration. The attendant with the stick was Ansumana Sherif, one of my students. The headpiece I am wearing is discussed in the December 20 letter home on Page 16. December 1970.

On June 25, 1970, I fell victim to malaria. About two weeks earlier I had stopped taking the recommended Peace Corps anti-malarial drug, Aralen. My left eye was experiencing repeated loss of vision for short periods of time, and I believed the blindness was a side effect of the drug. At the time, I was active with the Bo Boxing Club and the Bo Rugby Club. All of my rigorous activities plus teaching assignments, and the warm, humid tropical climate finally proved debilitating. At the first sign of symptoms, I visited the doctor at the Peace Corps Office and received a shot. This undoubtedly saved me from more serious trouble.

Home was just up the street, but by the time I reached the front door I barely had enough strength to fall into bed. As I lay there alone through the day and into the night, my head was spinning in a malarial fog. Fever and chills were relentless. About 8 p.m. the fever broke and my head felt a great relief. The next two days were devoted to rest.

After this experience, I obediently took an alternate anti-malarial drug but continued to have periodic episodes of blindness in the left eye for about five years.

The following letter and photographs reflect some of the other experiences I had in Sierra Leone. At the same time I was already planning my next request with the Peace Corps.

Letter Home
December 20, 1970
Bo Town, Sierra Leone

Dear Mother and Family,
    I hope the Christmas season is a merry one for you. I'm having a pleasant time in Bo Town, but I think I will write to the Thomas family in Taiama tomorrow and ask to visit them for Christmas.
    This year I danced for Ramadan instead of Christmas on December 1st. I went around to Muslim families, danced and gave balloons and candy. The janitor at our school, a Limba tribesman, made a new devil mask for me that fit my head much better than the one I wore last year for Christmas.
    Last week I was invited by Ken Jackson, geography instructor at Christ the King College, to accompany his student club on a study tour of Bonthe (Sherbro Island). We had a great time. The place is really isolated in the south of the country. If you look on the map, it looks like it broke away from the mainland, but really the island is built up from river sediments. No place on the island is more than 50 feet above sea level. We rented a launch for Le150 ($418 U.S.), and went around the island to the seaward side, then swam all day. The next day we took a launch that took us up the Wangie River to Gbundapi. The trip took 14 hours

---

of river travel. We slept on the launch. The next day we returned by road transport to Bo (Via Pujehun).

It may interest you to know that I might extend for a 3rd year in Sierra Leone, or transfer for a 3rd year volunteer work in British Honduras, Central America. I'll probably know where I'm going by February. Anyway, for sure I'll be home in July. I think I'll first visit Norway for my cousin's wedding, then to Illinois to look at the Eastern Illinois University campus, then to Albany, Oregon, and on down to Ontario. My plans are only in the thought stage.

I have not received many letters and think that some may have been censored. With this political trouble, much expatriate mail has been opened. I did get the *Daily Report* newspaper you mailed.

You know what I would appreciate? I would like information about Chaffey College and LaVerne College football this year. If you could get me a run down of the two teams I would be glad. Also, I have a friend who wants some stationery with flowers or some kind of pretty design on it. If you could buy a box (does not have to be special) and mail it slow mail, I would appreciate that.

With my second year, I notice I've gotten a bit apathetic about sending Christmas cards. I have not sent any at all. But I have gotten out the Christmas tree and fixed it up quite nicely.

I sent an article about rugby football to the *Daily Report* in Ontario. Did they print it? If they didn't, I'll tell you that I played in a national 7-a-side rugby tournament, and our team beat everyone

and won the tournament. We beat Freetown Rugby Club, Kono Rugby Club, Sierra Leone Army Rugby and the Marampa Mines Rugby Club.
Merry Christmas 1970.

It's your son,
Ted

Letter Home
March 1, 1971
Bo Town

Dear Mother and Family,
Plenty has happened since I wrote last.

I was relieved to hear the earthquake in California was not serious in Ontario. My housemate was listening to Voice of America the morning after the earthquake when I heard the words, "California earthquake." Even the British Broadcasting Corporation had a firsthand report.

You've probably heard that cholera has come to West Africa for the first time in history. The disease came out of India to East Africa, then via jet to Ghana before showing up in Sierra Leone. The country had mass vaccinations starting about six months ago. Well, many of these people don't realize that you still have to boil drinking water. Sure enough, about two weeks ago, a person with cholera shit in the Tia River, and hundreds of people all down the stream died. Mostly old people. Over sixty deaths in Taiama alone. Mr. Thomas and family were not affected. I think the tragedy shook the people in the area to start boiling their water.

Today was a big event in the country. It was a changeover from left to right hand driving. The advertising has been growing for the past few months regarding this day. From yesterday, February 28, at 10 p.m. until this morning at 6 a.m., nobody was allowed to drive on the streets. I saw one taxi driver yesterday about 7 p.m. driving down the middle of the street. This morning I was awakened by 6 a.m. There was a long caravan of cars going through town. All the drivers were giving a steady honking blast. People gathered to sit by the intersections watching police direct right hand traffic.

Last night when the curfew was in force, my good friend Prince Brima, who writes for the *Unity* newspaper, traveled in a special car, then called down to Freetown for a live interview on Radio Sierra Leone. I heard a similar fellow from Makeni earlier in the evening say (after being asked how the right hand driving was in Makeni), "Well, not much is happening, all is quiet." Not much he could say, considering no cars in the whole country were allowed on the streets.

There is too much to say in letters.
Love, Ted

P.S. The weather is too damn hot. I catch an hour nap in the afternoons, and sweat the whole time.

9. Bonthe Island. Christ the King College geographical club trip to Bonthe. The author is standing in the water at the bow. Club supervisor, Ken Jackson, is the first person standing on the bow. December 1970.

10. Bo Town. Kissy Town Road. The road sign is announcing nationwide right hand driving starting March 1, 1971. February 1971.

11. *Bo Town. Four friends left to right: Prince Brima, Kekura Bangura, PCV Bill Cernota and the author. 1970.*

Ken Jackson

12. *Bo Town. Cheerful leprous beggars approached in front of Choithram's Super Market. They suffered but had dignity. 1970.*

13. Bo Town. Bo School campus. The author volunteered as a coach and organizer for the Bo Boxing Club during 1970. On Boxing Day at the Bo School campus, he boxed Allie Bangura, the National Light-Middle Weight Champion, in a two round exhibition fight. To everyone's delight, Bangura gave this American a thorough beating. 1970.

14. *Marampa Mines Tournament. NATIONAL CHAMPIONS! The Bo Town Rugby Club won the National Seven-a-side Rugby Championship. Left to right: upper row, Labib Michael, Eddie Michael, PCV Bob Petterson, Father John O'Brien. Lower row, Father Lynch, Father Curran, Tony Rudge and the author. November 1970.*

April 19, 1971, was a day of celebration for Sierra Leone. That was the day the country officially became a republic, a day of pride for all Sierra Leoneans. I celebrated along with my friends.

Prince Brima

15. Bo Town. Bo School Band marching on Coronation Field to celebrate Independence Day just days after Sierra Leone became West Africa's newest republic. Replacing a sick student on the big drum is the author. April 27, 1971.

16. Bo Town. Sierra Leone Tenth Independence Day Celebration at Coronation Field. On the stand is Resident Minister of the Southern Province Mr. K. Conteh, who delivered a speech prepared by President Siaka P. Stevens, Sierra Leone's first president. April 27, 1971.

17. Bo Town. Torwama campus. President Siaka Stevens shaking hands with the author at the opening of the new campus of the Bo Teacher Training College. May 13, 1971.

Moving on to British Honduras

During my second year in Sierra Leone, I was encouraged to stay on a third year and work with the National Sports Council as a traveling track and field coach. Mr. Wallace-Johnson, Sports Council assistant director, proposed the position. An application was submitted, but not approved.

In June 1970 there were about 300 Peace Corps Volunteers serving in Sierra Leone when the Corps was hammered with negative articles printed in the national newspaper *Daily Mail*. The first in a series of editorial attacks began on June 3, 1970: "Today, we indict the American Peace Corps for the deteriorating standards of education, morals and discipline in Sierra Leone. . ." The basic idea was that there were too many Americans influencing the youth of Sierra Leone with American culture. The writer of the article considered this to be a negative situation. The entire hubbub didn't last long. There were even some really great rebuttal editorials defending the Peace Corps presence in competitive newspapers.

I am not sure if the negative articles contributed to my job request rejection, but the proposed position would have been highly visible, a situation that some might have wanted to avoid. Two Peace Corps Volunteer colleagues did extend their tenures for a third year at their respective schools in Bo.

In a subsequent conversation with Deputy Peace Corps Director for Sierra Leone, Sherwood 'Woody' Paulin, he mentioned that the British Honduras government in Central America had a standing request with the Peace Corps for a national track and field coach. He suggested I check the job out. Track and field had been part of my school life since 1960. I competed for nine years, from junior high through college.

The job prospect excited me, so I made contact with Peace Corps Washington, D.C., and Peace Corps British Honduras. In time, an invitation was offered for the position. The new assignment promised to be gratifying, almost like a paid vacation in paradise.

Below is a summary of the original request for a track and field director from the government of British Honduras to the United States Peace Corps:

Special Request Summary
Peace Corps, Washington

From the British Honduras Ministry of Local Government to the United States Peace Corps Request for a Coach, Track and Field Director:
PROJECT OBJECTIVES
1. To help the Government of British Honduras establish a track and field program.
2. To train counterpart coaches to insure the continuance of the program.
3. To organize competitions on an inter-school basis and organize sports clubs.
4. To establish a system of record keeping.
5. To help British Honduras to develop in its track and field potential to the point that international and Olympic competition is feasible.

The British Honduras government wanted programs that promoted a national outlook among the people. Athletics was one great medium to strive towards that goal.

On June 10, 1971, I became an official transfer volunteer to the self-governing colony of British Honduras. My transfer had been approved! The job was going to be a very good adventure. All I had to do was reach out.

Soon I found myself departing Sierra Leone for the last time, leaving from the Lungi International Airport near Freetown.[2]

1
Notes

[1] The use of the word *devil* for Sierra Leone masked dancers is a poor translation to English for what these characters actually stand for. Foreigners undoubtedly gave the misleading label to these traditional characters many years ago. The devil dancers of Sierra Leone are not evil. They come from a West African tradition of secular spirits that were often characters of important energy, serving various functions such as protector, bearer of good luck, ancestral keeper and participants in ceremony or dancing for amusement. Masked devils also play a prominent role for Sierra Leone secret societies, helping to train young people to be good citizens. www.randafricanart.com/Mende-mask - SierraLeoneHeritage.org –glossary – devil.

[2] Less than twenty miles from Lungi International Airport is Bunce Island on the Sierra Leone River. In 1670, a fortified British slave market was established on the island and remained in business for about 140 years. During the eighteenth century, slaves in transit at Bunce were sold mostly to locations in the Caribbean and the American South. It is likely that ancestors of Belize Creoles last saw African shores when leaving this dreadful outpost on their 50-day hellish "Middle Passage" to the Caribbean.

When down on luck, John Newton, the author of *Amazing Grace,* and himself a slave trader for nine years, lived near Bunce Island for two years of difficult bondage to a female African master.

2
Welcome to British Honduras

My initial training for service in British Honduras took place with sixteen other trainees in Ponce, Puerto Rico, beginning July 1971. As in Sierra Leone, training was strong in language and cross-cultural classes. Spanish classes lasted eight hours a day for six weeks.[1] Following our arrival in Belize City on August 29, orientation continued two more weeks.

Earlier in 1971, Alex Frankson, a retired civil servant, was appointed Peace Corps Country Director of British Honduras. He was a Jamaican national who had lived and worked in the country since 1937.[1]

Alex had the distinction of being the only Peace Corps director in the world who was not an American citizen. Since British Honduras was a colony of England, the country had a U.S. consulate rather than a U.S. embassy. Had there been an embassy, the Peace Corps director's post would have required a high-level security clearance, in order to participate in internal and sensitive meetings. High-level security clearances were unavailable to non-U.S. citizens.[2]

18. Belize City. Peace Corps Director Alex Frankson. 1972.

19. Belize City. Norman, Belizean Peace Corps driver, with Associate Peace Corps Director Kelly Compton (seated). 1972.

Ted W. Cox

20. *Belize City. Peace Corps Office Administrator Barbara Harris. 1972.*

Rob Thurston

21. *Near Belize City. Peace Corps Associate Director Rob Thurston landing a barracuda. 1972.*

Ex PCV Andy Witthohn, a short-term contract trainer for our group had just completed two years volunteer service in Belize City teaching at Belize Junior Secondary School. Andy showed me around, taking special pride in his mastery of Creole whenever possible. I told him how surprised I was to find the Creole of Belize so similar to the Krio spoken in Sierra Leone.

One afternoon Andy took me to visit a volunteer who was a patient at Holden Memorial Hospital. PCV Joe Maryski, a recreation director at Stafford Youth Club in Belize City, was recovering from injuries received in a deadly auto accident on August 20.[3] Joe was traveling with twenty-seven Belizeans to participate in a Guatemalan competition when an oncoming vehicle, hauling a protruding tractor blade, fatally slashed their truck. This occurred only eight miles from the Guatemalan border on the Western Highway. Four of the athletes died at the scene. Joe eventually recovered from injuries and continued his service at the youth center.[4]

Andy related that some volunteers were betting my job would end in frustration and failure. They believed the position was doomed from the start because there was not enough work for a track coach. The comment did not mean much to me. My head was full of ideas beyond sitting at a desk waiting for track and field season to roll around.

Letter Home
September 9, 1971
Belize City

Dear Mom and Family,
 I am going on my second week in Belize City (arrived August 29th).
 British Honduras is great. Belize City has one big problem though - open sewers. Other than that, the place is positively interesting.
 Last weekend our Peace Corps training group went up-country to a place called Central Farm (government operated). From there we went to the Mountain Pine Ridge where we visited a ranch owned by an American. With all the pine trees and horses you would think that we were in the U.S.A. The next day we went west and saw some Mayan ruins built about 900 A.D.

On Monday, I was dropped off in the new capital city of Belmopan. There I met the man who will be my boss for the next two years, Minister of Local Government the Hon. Louis Sylvestre, along with his permanent secretary and the assistant secretary. The minister said that I was the expert and that he would wait for my recommendations. My office will be in Belize City at the Ministry of Community and Social Development.

During the next month I will be traveling around the country getting familiar with the needs of my work.

This Sunday I will be interviewed on the national radio to let people know of my job and what I am doing here.

Love, Teddy

Ted W. Cox

22. Cayo District. Xunantunich Mayan Ruins. Trainees visit the site during in-country training. September 1971.

On Monday, September 6, I made my first official trip to the new capital, Belmopan, where I met with the minister of local government, Honorable Louis Sylvestre, and his assistant Permanent Secretary Carl Coleman. In the brief meeting, Minister Sylvestre said that he would rely on my recommendations as to how to proceed with the job, and that I would answer directly to Mr. Coleman.

This meeting was important and I would work hard to keep their support. Direct access to the minister's office gave me leverage in performing the job, which saved time. Working within the framework of the system, you were expected to follow the chain of command when submitting projects or else risk making life difficult for yourself. In my case, the link was direct to the permanent secretary of the minister, skipping over the social development officer and her assistant.

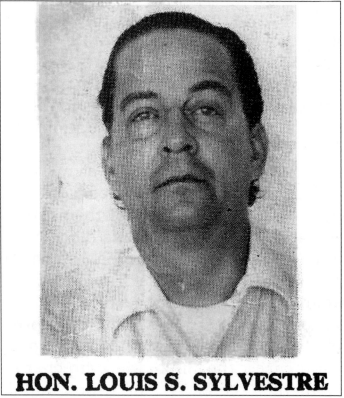

HON. LOUIS S. SYLVESTRE

23. Minister of Local Government, Community and Social Development. September 1971.

To get the ball rolling, I mentioned to Mr. Coleman that I would like to visit the various secondary schools in Belize City. The following day, I had in hand an official letter of introduction that could be used when making contacts.

P. O. Box 2246
Telephones: 2236 & 2257.
Please Quote
Reference No.

MINISTRY OF LOCAL GOVERNMENT,
COMMUNITY AND SOCIAL
DEVELOPMENT,
BELIZE CITY.

7th September, 1971.

To Whom it may Concern

        The bearer of this note is Mr. Theodore Cox (he would prefer if you call him Ted) who is a Peace Corp Volunteer attached to the Ministry of Local Government, Community and Social Development.

        His Official title is Coach and Athletic Diretor and he is here in this Country to endeavour to improve the standard of Athletics (especially Track and Field).

        He will endeavour to carry out his duties by working in co-ordination with the local Amateur Athletic Association and the Schools.

        The Ministry would be most grateful for any assistance which could be given to him.

(C. C. Coleman)
for Ag. Permanent Secretary
(Local Government)

24. Introduction letter from the Ministry of Local Government.

Although the minister of education, the Honorable Guadalupe Pech, was aware of my new post in the country, I had not yet met with him. To establish a direct contact was a courtesy and also important. Leni Jo Usher, an English teacher at St. John's College, offered to make introductions. The day she took me to see the minister, he was at his office in Belize City. Following introductions and a brief conversation he assured me that I was welcome to proceed with cooperation from his ministry. Inter-ministry cooperation was important if work was to proceed smoothly.

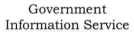

Government
Information Service

HON. GUADALUPE PECH

25. Minister of Education.
September 1971.

2
Notes

[1] A.S. Frankson, *A Caribbean Identity: Memoirs of the Colonial Service* (London: The Radcliffe Press, 2008).

[2] Rob Thurston, telephone interview by the author, June 10, 2013.

[3] Evan X Hyde, e-mail to author, April 28, 2014. (Hyde contributed PCV Joe Maryski's name.)

[4] Evan X Hyde, *Sports, Sin and Subversion* (Belize City: Ramos Publishing, 2008).

3
A Stormy Start

Edith was the strongest hurricane to form during the 1971 season and it was headed our way! During my first week in the country we followed its progress, which gave us an exciting baptism on the colony's National Day, September 10. The day before, Edith had intensified to a powerful Category 5 with 160 mph winds before making landfall on northeastern Nicaragua. In Nicaragua it rapidly weakened over the mountainous terrain and emerged into the Gulf of Honduras as a Category 3.

Letter Home
September 20, 1971
Belize City

Dear Mom and Family,
Hurricane Edith gave quite a fright to people around here. She passed by on September 10, which is this country's National Day. There are big, big celebrations during National Day.
I got out of bed at 5 a.m. on the 10th, to help layout the MCC Grounds for a track and field meet that afternoon. By 10 a.m. we were half finished with the preparations, when we saw the red flag go up with a black dot. That basically means you better be ready for trouble, so we abandoned our efforts. People were still celebrating in the streets up to that time, but at seven o'clock when that

second flag went up on public buildings, people left the streets like a bomb was coming. They were encouraged to go to hurricane shelters and the strongest buildings.

As the hurricane was bearing down on Belize City, Premier George Price finished his National Day speech at Memorial Park. Prior to his address, the talk of the town was that he planned to make an important statement. Price wanted to declare that British Honduras would be renamed Belize in 1972, a gesture to remove the sound of colonial dependency. What the public did not know was that the British Foreign Office in London had blocked the premier from making such a specific proclamation. Leaders in England suspected imminent hostility from Guatemala and judged that the timing of such an announcement might trigger an invasion of the colony at the very time that the garrison was undermanned. The British supported the name change, but the timing was wrong in their opinion.

In 1964, British Honduras had achieved internal self-government, while Great Britain retained control of the country's defense, foreign affairs, and internal security.[1]

During 1970 and 1971, Guatemala had been conducting intimidating military maneuvers along the border, including photograph reconnaissance via a high flyover of Belize City. Plans were just being made to reinforce the garrison, as the Guatemalan threat remained at an ever-present high.

When Premier Price gave his speech, it was modified to say that the coming year would "most likely" be the right time to change the name of the country.

From the sports field I went to my room at the Hiltown Hotel, to see what was happening. Trainees were packing and readying to go to the U.S. Consulate where we were told to go in case of a hurricane. I showered and followed them. Everybody brought his or her bottle of rum, since it was national day and we had expected to celebrate. I stopped by a store that was closing and bought my own bottle of Belizean rum.

As the night advanced, Radio Belize reports got grimmer, and we expected the worst. A six-foot tidal wave was predicted for later that night.

If a six-foot tidal surge had arrived, it would have breached the city's storm walls and flooded the town with about three feet or so of ocean water.

That night a platoon of soldiers was positioned at the nearby sturdy Pallotti Convent. They were assigned anti-looting duty if a disaster occurred. A special hurricane committee gathered at the police strong house downtown to oversee emergency arrangements. They followed the storm's movements through contact with the hurricane center in Miami. Radio Belize kept the public informed with regular broadcasts.

The consul general was a good host to the volunteers who showed up for shelter. We drank our rum while he got out "C" rations and regaled us with stories of his days in the Dominican Republic during a period of political turmoil in 1965. Before I fell asleep on the dining room floor, about 8:30 p.m., I heard Radio Belize announce that a six-foot tidal wave was expected to hit later that night.

By 2 a.m., while I was sleeping, the hurricane took a sharp turn north of Belize City, making landfall with tropical storm winds of 70 mph. I woke up about 4 a.m. and realized most of the volunteers had gone back to the hotel, so I left too.

During a 2012 telephone conversation with fellow PCV Neal Hammond, who was also at the consulate that night, he commented:

Neal: I remember that the predictions were that this was going to be a violent Category 3 hurricane. We all went over to the consulate to wait out the hurricane. When it finally hit it was like a tropical storm. Edith turned out to be more like a big bluster for us. When the wind died down a lot of us left and went back to the hotel.

The following week a letter addressed to all Peace Corps Volunteers was sent to the Peace Corps Office from the consul's wife, stating that in the future no booze could be brought into the consulate during an emergency. Any alcohol would be impounded. The letter also suggested that, if possible, we should find refuge elsewhere. Of course, I was asleep by 8:30, but the other volunteers said she was making a fuss out of very little. Considering that we were guests, and that there was at least one cigarette burn in her rug, it's obvious we should have used better judgment.

In 1961, Hurricane Hattie had devastated Belize City with fierce winds and a series of 12-foot tidal waves that breached the city's sea wall. It sent 10-foot gushes of water through the streets, tearing 75% of the city apart. The surge reached as far as five miles inland. When I arrived ten years later, there were still cockeyed buildings and crooked cisterns as lingering proof.

But I had not made friends yet with any Belizeans who would have told me just how bad things could be. Being from Southern California, I just didn't understand the danger. The storm seemed a novelty to me. Wind comes, then rain, then sun, and then rain and wind again and, finally, the tidal wave, which we fortunately did not experience.

3
Notes

[1] The Belizean government had a tiny defense force that was virtually run on a part-time basis. The local militia was not capable of successfully defending the country on its own strength at that time.

4
Belize City Life

In 1971, British Honduras had been a self-governing colony for only seven years with a small but ethnically diverse population of 120,000.

At that time, the Creole inhabitants, many of whom were a mixture of African, European and Spanish ancestry, accounted for approximately fifty-two percent of the country's residents. Twenty-two percent were Mestizo, a mixture of Spanish and Indian ancestry. Mayan Indians represented approximately thirteen percent; and the Garifuna[1], seven percent. Another seven percent of the population was a variety of East Indian, Lebanese, Chinese and Caucasian descent, including Mennonite immigrants from the U.S. and Canada.[2]

Belize City was the country's main cultural and commercial hub. In heart and soul, Belize City was and still is a Caribbean city. Most people living there speak both English and Creole.

The population of Belize City in 1971 was 39,000 and growing. This number equaled one-third of the country's total inhabitants. No other urban area at that time had a population of more than a few thousand.

Belize City covered just four square miles on low-lying and reclaimed land scarcely eighteen inches above sea level. Haulover Creek, the river along which the town stands, bisects the city into a north side and south side. Surrounding the town is mangrove swamp and the Caribbean Sea.

26. Belize City. Entrance to Haulover Creek. October 1971.

27. Belize City. Victoria Street as seen from my friend Frank Cervantes' home. 1973.

Infrogmation (Wikimedia Commons)

28. Belize City. Craig Street, the neighborhood of my Belizean friend Dave Anderson from 1945 to 1961. 1975.

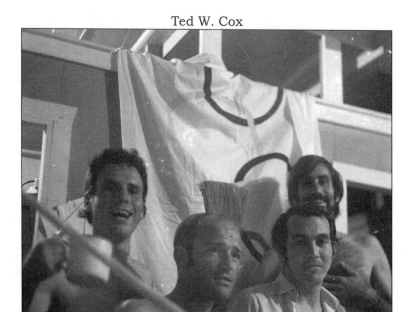

29. *Belize City. Four friends, left to right: Jerry Conroy (Irish volunteer), the author, Frank Cervantes, PCV Rick Sharp. Note the typical inside wall construction that is open on top. May 15, 1973.*

Cisterns for collecting personal use rainwater were located in many yards. Some sat out of line, a result of Hurricane Hattie.

Many homes were raised on stilts from two to seven feet offering limited protection from heavy rain drainage and minor storm surges. Other houses were built in colonial style from the ground up. Most had corrugated-iron roofs. Inside the houses were partition walls constructed of wallboard panels that did not extend to the ceiling, allowing circulation but limited privacy.

Because of the swampy nature of the Belize delta, drainage canals were dug, crossing the town to the sea. These projects predated 1810 when a twenty-two-foot canal was completed on the south side of town. In 1817 a nine-foot canal was dug on the north side. Other canal projects include the Collet Canal, completed in 1919 to meet the needs of expansion.[3]

Belize Institute of Social Research and Action

30. Belize City. East Canal Street. 1915.

31. Belize City. Eve Street Canal from North Front Street to the sea, also referred to in Creole as "Dead house kinel." 1975.

The high water table in Belize City prevented pit latrine construction. So waterways received chamber-pot contents from homes that could not afford enclosed septic tanks. These drops were only allowed at night. Predictably, the open sewers produced stench around the canals that grew stronger during the dry season.[4]

By the mid-1930s, indoor sanitation and septic tanks became standard construction in middle and upper class homes. Yet indoor plumbing and septic tanks remained out of reach for many landlords and poor homeowners unable to afford such luxury.

The two rental homes I lived in during my time in Belize both had indoor plumbing. At the first rental, on Baymen Avenue, the girlfriend of my roommate came to town for a visit during March 1972. Late one night I woke to sounds of panic from the bathroom and made a quick dash to see what was up. It turned out the lady had unwittingly sat down on the toilet only to hear scratching on the porcelain inside the bowl. A quick peek revealed that a land crab had made its way up the sewer line to pay a visit. At that time, there was no city sewage-pipe system. Our house had a septic tank apparently with drainage tiles. How else could a crab get into the tank?

Many septic tanks were sealed because of the shallow seawater table. They had to be pumped out as needed, at expense to the owner.

* * * * *

Haulover Creek (a river) separates Belize City into a north and a south side. In 1923 a swing bridge, constructed in England, was assembled over the river. The new bridge replaced a non-swinging overpass. Four men manually opened and closed the bridge twice a day, once in the morning and once in the evening, allowing boat traffic to move freely. Movement by pedestrians and traffic at the bridge came to a standstill as people impatiently waited for boats to pass and the bridge to close. Photo 32 was taken from North Front Street looking south to Albert Street while the bridge was being closed clockwise. The long line of pedestrians on the left wait to cross.

Ted W. Cox

32. Belize City. Four men closing the swing bridge on a September afternoon. 1971.

33. *Belize City Public Market, located next to the swing bridge on Haulover Creek. Today, a two-story building called the Commercial Center sits on this location. 1972.*

34. *Belize City. Haulover Creek. Premier George Price had his office on the second floor of the government building on the right. The distant building on the far left is the Bliss Institute. 1972.*

35. Belize City. Masonic burial procession next to St. Mary's Hall. September 1971.

In one sense, a walk through any neighborhood in the early evening was like a stroll through a large shopping mall. The same reggae[5] or holiday music could be heard from one house to another, echoing up and down the street. That's because everyone was tuned to the only broadcast station available, Radio Belize; and there was no T.V.

Then there was radio commentator Eddie Seferino Coleman, the beloved voice of Radio Belize. For years he hosted a spellbinding morning show that touched the hearts of Belizeans nationwide. Eddie Coleman drew the people of Belize together each morning when the station came on air. With enduring charisma, and a unique brand of humor, Eddie ran through a verbal wake-up call to every corner of the country, rapidly jabbering among Creole, English and Spanish. "Good Morning, Belize City; Good Morning, Stann Creek; Good Morning, Punta Gorda; Good Morning, Belmopan; Good Morning, Corozal; Good Morning, Orange Walk; Good Morning, Cayo." Eddie was always coming up with personal comments for anyone listening. No matter how remote the area, he could find you. Each and every corner of Belize was singled out. Coleman was phenomenal. "This is Radio Belize, jewel in the heart of the Caribbean basin. Esta es Radio Belice, la joya en el corazon de la cuenca del Caribe." Or something very similar to that.

An economic shot in the arm for Belize City was witnessed at the beginning of each month when lines gathered at the General Post Office (and probably other POs around the country). People were seen waiting to cash money orders from family members working outside the country, mostly in the United States, and totaling over $200,000 a month. About 25,000 Belizeans lived legally, and a few thousand illegally, in the United States at the time. The British forces also injected one to two million dollars each year into the local economy.[6] Soldiers stationed at the Airport Camp were often in town when not out on exercises. Since the total national budget of British Honduras at the time was about thirty million dollars, these monetary infusions made a big impact.[7]

* * * * *

Ted W. Cox

36. *Belize City. View of Government Customs Building. The boat pictured was named* Maya Prince *and made roundtrip runs from Belize City to Punta Gorda. June 16, 1973.*

Although Belize City was the population center of the country, there was no large source of industrial employment in the area. As a result, the unemployment rate was high. The government employed many folks in the civil service, there were other, typical private-sector jobs available, and the port of Belize had a busy waterfront. But those with no steady employment had to be inventive to make ends meet.

One way of generating cash was selling goods. The shortage of employment opportunities contributed to an abundance of tiny shops and street vendors in Belize City such as the one described to me by Dave Anderson:

Dave: There used to be an old man by the name of Mr. Marin in Belize City. He had a cart that he pushed and he did business mostly during the school day. He would go in front of the gates of Holy Redeemer Boys and Girls Elementary School on North Front Street right next to Holy Redeemer Cathedral. Mr. Marin made empanadas at his home and sold them to the school children off his cart, also powder buns, fresco (snow cone), and ganachos (fried tortillas with cheese and beans) and local candy. He would bring these things ready made from his home, keep them warm in a pan, with just enough that the kids would buy him out during recess time.[8]

There were also a series of about nine makeshift shops located along Haulover Creek, between Victoria and Pickstock on North Front Street. They sold local candy by the piece and single cigarettes, fresh fruit and soft drinks. Some would bake bread right there in small amounts, creole bread and creole bun, which was sweetened with brown sugar. Some of these shops doubled as living quarters.

Ted W. Cox

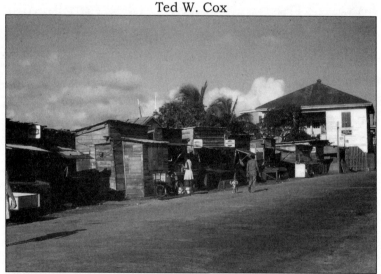

37. Belize City. Shanty shops located on North Front Street. 1975.

38. Belize City. Drying laundry behind shanty shops on North Front Street. The houses across Haulover Creek are located on Regent Street West. 1975.

On the other side of the river, anyone could rent a stall in the public market and sell goods as basic as cigarettes, matches and chewing gum.

Entrepreneurs also made money by selling lottery tickets, guiding tourists and scalping movie tickets.

39. Belize City. National Stadium during horse racing day. The vendor is selling peeled oranges. April 29, 1973.

Speaking of lottery, every weeknight the streets were filled with people buying the popular Boledo lottery tickets. This type of gaming was introduced through radio broadcasts in the mid-1940s from the Sunday Panama national lottery. That's when Belizeans began listening on the radio and organizing bets.

By 1947, Belizeans were playing their own lottery, the Boledo lottery. The bet consisted of numbers between 00 and 99.

One chance of two combined numbers was purchased for five cents. A winning ticket paid $3.50 B.H. On Sundays there was the Jack Pot lottery. Those tickets cost ten cents for three numbers between 0000 and 9999, with the highest payoff being $150 B.H.

Lottery was exciting and many people pooled their money to purchase sheets of ten or more tickets.[9] Some people used "Dream Books" to compile numbers. A book might associate numbers with the human body. For example, if you had a dream that involved some part of the body, the book gave that body part a number that could be used when playing the lottery. In addition, say your aunt got some kind of sickness, the condition would relate to a specific number. "Ah dream that Auntie me get wan heart attack and den ker-uh da hospital."
("I dreamed that my aunt had a heart attack and was taken to the hospital.") So, you'd look up the number that represented your aunt's heart attack.

Merchants and Boledo associations ran the game at that time. Many street sellers were individuals who got ten percent on tickets sold and fifteen percent if they did not sell the winning number. The consumer, when purchasing a ticket on the street, would automatically check the valid date on the back of the ticket before buying. Dishonest hustlers were known to sell outdated tickets to unsuspecting buyers and make off with the loot.

Some social life in Belize City revolved around private parties. There was also a variety of drinking establishments that fit different income budgets. Peace Corps Volunteers were usually close to broke, which limited their options.[10] Many off-duty soldiers spent time at the popular Bamboo Bay Nightclub on Regent Street West. Owned by Danny Weir, the club's second floor extended a bit over Haulover Creek. If you tossed food scraps out the window into the waters below, government-protected catfish would be observed eating the food in frenzy on the surface. The catfish's local claim to fame was that they were efficient night scavengers, cleaning up raw sewage.

Also popular in town were public dances, social clubs, athletic events and movie theatres.

40. Belize City. Postal Inspector Gilmore Hinkson, left, and Bill Lightburn on a corner by the swing bridge talking sports and politics. Losing Boledo tickets litter the ground by their feet! December, 1975.

41. Belize City. Four friends, from left: the author, Kelly Compton, Henry, and Leroy. Many good times were spent at Kelly's house during my first nine months in-country. March 12, 1972.

On the underbelly of Belize City were two brothels. The Continental, referred to as the Big 'C', was on Freetown Road. Another one was located on New Road behind businessman Santiago Castillo's office.

In 1981, a third house of ill repute, called the Rose Garden, opened near Mile 8 on the Northern Highway. Raul Aguilar owned that business. Mainly soldiers frequented this brothel, located near Airport Camp. Prostitutes were called "fallen birds" from Honduras, Salvador, and Guatemala.

One good thing about these establishments, patronized by soldiers, was that the Army medic would give a medical check up at the businesses at least once a month. If an employee was diagnosed with venereal disease and continued to practice, the doctor would tell the owner, "Look, we will forbid our soldiers from coming here." So, as the story goes, the owners kept a tight rein on their employees. If workers became infected, they weren't allowed to work their trade.

Royal Highland Fusiliers.org.uk

42. Belize District. The Rose Garden was located between mile seven and nine on the Northern Highway.

* * * * *

On Monday, May 29, 1972, my Belizean friend Frank Cervantes and I planned to see a movie downtown while the political party UBAD (United Black Association for Development) was having a peaceful march. Organizers were issued a permit for the gathering and were protesting, among other things, Guatemala's claim to Belize. The march turned into a riot when some participants started stoning the Guatemalan Consulate on Albert Street. For a time the rioters were out of control. Then the Police Special Force Unit arrived and began using tear gas.[11] Before we knew it, Frank and I were in the tear gas cloud. There were a number of storefronts with broken windows.

As the local militia began making arrests, some rioters ducked into the Palace Theatre, pursued by a member of the riot squad who proceeded to toss a can of tear gas. The result was a panic among moviegoers who trampled each other as they ran for the exits. Frank and I got out of the area and decided our best option was to head for home. The Palace Theatre, oldest cinema in Belize City, was where Frank and I had planned to go that night. Lucky for us we missed the incident inside the theatre.

43. Ladyville. Police Special Force Unit Corporal Bob Moriano leading children's activities. August 1972.

4
Notes

[1] The Garifuna people are descendants of runaway African slaves who intermingled with Carib and Arawak Indians on the Island of St. Vincent during the sixteenth century.

[2] Vin H. Lawrence, *National Youth Programme: Youth in Belize Moving Towards Development* (Belize City: Government Printers, December 1972).

[3] John Everitt, "The Growth and Development of Belize City," *Belizean Studies* (Volume 14, No. 1), 1986.

[4] At times over the years Belize City has received downbeat comments regarding canal stench. A visitor will find similar odor nuisance in places like the narrow canals of Venice or on the waters of Hong Kong Harbor.

[5] Some of my favorite tunes from 1971 to 1973 included 1971 Jamaican Music Festival Winner "Cherry Oh Baby" by Eric Donaldson; "Flying Machine," version by Teddy Mangus; "Sorry for Maga Dog," version by Peter Tosh; "Love of the Common People," version by Eric Donaldson; "Macabee Version," by Max Romeo; "Stir It Up," and "I Can See Clearly Now," by Johnny Nash. Check out these tunes on YouTube for a nostalgic visit to the past.

[6] These monetary estimates are taken from notes I placed in my journal in May 1973. At the time I failed to indicate the source of this information.

[7] Norman Fairweather, WGBX Boston, Public Access Channel, 1973. In 1972, half of the Belizean national budget was used to pay teacher and public employee salaries.

8 Dave Anderson, telephone interview by the author, June 21, 2013.

9 Mary Kenyon-Bullard, "The Recognition of Psychiatric Disorder in British Honduras" (PhD diss., University of Oregon, March 1973).

10 The Peace Corps Director, Alex Frankson, set the living allowance for Volunteers equal to or just above the average Belizean salary, about $95 U.S. per month. Living on such a tight budget limited what we could do in the community. I did receive remuneration from the ministry when working in the districts to pay for food and travel.

11 The Police Special Force Unit was a paramilitary organization used not only for military duties but also as the local riot squad for the country.

5
Belmopan

Because of the destruction to Belize City by Hurricane Hattie in 1961, a decision was made to move the colony's capital fifty miles west, to the middle of the country, high and dry from the threat of Caribbean tidal surges. Belmopan, the name chosen for the new capital, was built from scratch beginning in 1967 and opened for occupation in August 1970 (Map E, Page 143). It was literally carved out of the jungle as bulldozers leveled everything into a field of rubble prior to construction. Only a few magnificent trees were left in the open spaces to suggest the original jungle canopy height.

The first stage of development was largely accomplished with British grants and loans totaling about $14 million U.S.[1] The capital was a cause of great pride for Premier George Price, who was one of the first to take up residence there.

44. Belmopan in 1970. The new capital, with all its raw edges, is ready for settlement.
(#1) Belmopan Comprehensive School. (#2) Ring Road surrounding most of the original capital.

(#3) Premier George Prices's house. (#4) The Ecumenical Center. (#5) Mahogany tree. (#6) Government offices. (#7) National Assembly Building. (#8) Belize House, the governor's residence.

45. Belmopan. Old-growth mahogany tree (#5) in field near Premier George Price's house. 1971.

46. *Belmopan. At work in the Social Development Department (#6). Lee Gill in back, Darius Martinez in center and Mary Jane Robb at right. Mary Jane was a 4-H Volunteer from Michigan.* [2] *1972.*

47. Belmopan. The third house from the left was Premier George Price's home (#3). The odd-shaped building was the Ecumenical Center (#4) where Methodists, Anglicans and Catholics took turns in worship. The Methodists and Catholics now have their own buildings. Today this building is St. Ann's Anglican Church. 1972.

When I arrived in 1971, the population of Belmopan was roughly 3,000. Planners envisioned a city of 30,000 by 1990,[3] but in 2013 there was about half that number. In 1971, many civil servants struggled with isolation in the jungle capital. For many others, their life, culture and dreams were firmly in Belize City, so they commuted. Every workday, Monday through Friday, these people traveled in unorganized caravans for a fifty-mile drive over an unpaved but well graded highway. Vehicles sped along, skipping over the corrugated road at fifty-plus miles per hour for a smoother ride. The challenge was keeping the dust off yourself and enduring the washboard effect. The washboard was a wave-like pattern commonly seen on unpaved roads. Tires shifted gravel at certain speeds, causing the series of regular bumps and shallow dips across the roadbed. Regular grading by the public works department temporarily eliminated the condition while preventing potholes and water erosion from rain. The trick for a smooth ride was to time your driving speed so that your tires would hit only the top of the bumps.

48. Belmopan. Side road off Ring Road. The author took this picture of a 50-mph speed limit sign ushering motorists into the jungle. Was the sign dedicated to an optimistic road expansion plan in the near future? 1973.

5
Notes

[1] Louis De La Haba, "Belize, The Awakening Land," *National Geographic* (January 1972).
The Baron Bliss Trust Fund helped to purchase the land upon which Belmopan was built.
[2] Mary Jane Robb was the 1972-73 delegate to Belize as a 4-H Youth Volunteer sponsored by the International Farm Youth Exchange and Youth Development Program. She assisted professional and volunteer leaders in Belize, conducting educational programs, recruiting and training leaders, organizing new clubs and promoting community service programs. During the 1972 National Agricultural Show in Belmopan, she coordinated the program crowning Miss Agriculture Belize.
[3] De La Haba, 134.

6
Getting to Work

Ted W. Cox

49. Belize City. The author's first day on the job as Track and Field Director at the old Social Development Department Office on Daly Street. September 1971.

Working at the Social Development Department in Belize City was great because it was filled with interesting and motivated people. The department was established in 1944 to undertake co-ordination of social welfare throughout the colony. Prior to that, churches and other voluntary organizations provided social welfare.

The team I worked around dealt with all ages and included childcare and matrimonial problems, delinquents, unemployment, probation services, assistance for poverty burials and cottage industries. Out of town, the department co-operated with village councils, taking an active role in various committees.

Ted W. Cox

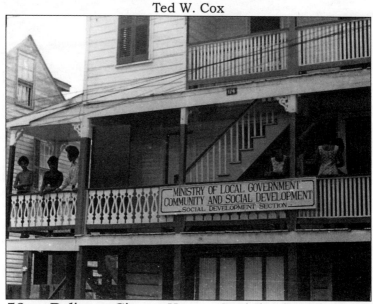

50. *Belize City. New Social Development Department Offices on Church Street. May 1973.*

My work was strictly related to track and field. In 1956 the British Honduras Amateur Athletic Association (BHAAA) was formed and for about ten years made progress in the sport. But then apathy set in and athletics went into a decline. I was charged with bringing Belizeans together by weaving the athletic tradition into a new life. Luckily for me, the locals were happy and excited to have a grassroots coach in the community.

As high school classes started in September, I proceeded to visit each school to make my introduction and find out what sport facilities were available in Belize City. After a few sweat-filled days walking about, I purchased a bicycle with discretionary funds available from the Peace Corps Office. The bike was a big help.[1] When meeting a principal, I first presented the introductory letter from the ministry.

For three months I was busy getting to know people and how I could best be of service. Belize had a tradition of track meets going back to the 1920s that celebrated the people's independent spirit. I learned this from Belizean sports historian Bill Lightburn.

Towards the end of my service in Belize, Bill and I carried out interviews with elderly Belizean athletes. One day we visited Walter Bennett at his house on King Street.

Due to a stroke, Bennett was unable to talk, but radiated excitement as Bill spoke about the 10th of September track and field meets of his youth. Mr. Bennett proudly displayed prizes won during those years.

Ted W. Cox

51.Belize City. Walter Bennett with prizes he won as an athlete during the 1920s 10th of September competitions. June 22, 1973.

Letter Home
October 18, 1971
Belize City

Dear Mother and Family,
I received two letters from you today. I also received the track and field rulebook last Friday. The rulebook came just in time. I didn't have one until then, and we had a track meet just yesterday (the one that was postponed September 10 due to the hurricane). The meet lasted all day and was a success, but went too slow. I took some pictures at the meet and will send you some.
I was interviewed again on Radio Belize, talking about the track meet and what I was doing.
The weather has been cooling off and rain has been more frequent, but today is hot.
I got a letter from Neil. He say's he doesn't write because nothing happens. Well, I know that is baloney since he travels around doing things.
It's your son,
Love, Teddy

Besides visiting Belize City schools, I surveyed the MCC Grounds and took an inventory of all track and field equipment on hand. The field was originally built as a cricket pitch in the mid-1950s. Before the MCC Grounds was developed, the land it sat on was property of the crown colony. Local Government Minister Albert Cattouse was instrumental in obtaining the property for the development.[2]

In early April 1960 the world famous Marylebone Cricket Club from England was on a West Indies tour and came to Belize City to play two matches against local teams. The competitions were held at the MCC Grounds. The field was apparently named at that time to honor the club's historic visit.[3]

Use of the MCC Grounds was in demand and could pose scheduling challenges between track and field, soccer and softball. In addition, the field was only large enough to accommodate a 300-meter running track. I discovered that critical markers used to lay out the field were missing. Bill Lightburn noticed that track records over the previous few years showed unusually slow times, compared to earlier performances. We suspected an inaccurately marked field was the cause.

Report to Minister Hon. Louis Sylvestre
December 20, 1971

In early September 1971 I discovered that 4 of the 6 iron rod markers buried to mark the location of turning points for the 300-meter track at the MCC Grounds were missing. These points were of major importance for the accurate layout of the track. With the assistance of the survey department, two Peace Corps surveyors helped to locate these points. We then drove new locator rods into the ground.

Ted W. Cox

52. Belize City. MCC Grounds. PCV Herb Kroehl watches groundskeeper Terrance Jones drive a permanent rod used to mark the location of turning points for the 300-meter track.
October 14, 1971.

53. MCC Grounds. PCV Neil Policelli surveying markers for the 300-meter track. October 14, 1971.

6
Notes

[1] Six months later, I used a chunk of my Peace Corps vacation allowance (about $100 U.S.) and bought a Honda 50 from a Belizean named Robert Jones. This turned out to be a bad idea. Within a few weeks the motorcycle broke down, needing major repairs. I eventually junked the vehicle, ending my idea of independent mobility. The poor decision made a trip to California difficult until I secured part time work during the vacation (Chapter 20).

[2] A.S. Frankson, *A Caribbean Identity: Memoirs of the Colonial Service* (London: The Radcliffe Press, 2008).

[3] On April 2, 1960, Marylebone beat the British Honduras Governor's XI team by 218 runs (278 to 60). On April 4, Marylebone won a second match by 163 runs (277 to 114).

7
Garifuna Settlement Days 1971

During my first day of work at the Social Development Department I met Darius Martinez, who was from Stann Creek, Southern District. The day was also his first on the job. He was a new welfare officer and would soon be helping the very poor in Belize City, as well as counseling juvenile delinquents. His other responsibilities included community development in rural areas.

In order to take this job, Darius had to leave his wife, Therese, in Stann Creek and rent an apartment in Belize City for about $50 U.S. a month. They soon bought a house in Belmopan where Darius and Therese moved after about a year and where they still reside as of this publication.

We became immediate friends and he invited me to visit Stann Creek (soon to be renamed Dangriga) to celebrate the Garifuna Settlement Days on the weekend of November 19. This event was started in 1941 to celebrate the arrival of the Garifuna people from Honduras as refugees to Stann Creek in 1832.[1] Darius's mother was one of the charter organizers of the yearly celebration.

The Garifuna people differ from the Creole population by reason of having their own history, traditions and language.

In 1971, the anniversary day fell on a Friday. Darius and I left Belize City Friday after work, taking a public transport. When we entered Stann Creek Town, there was a different feel in the air. I could sense that their cultural traditions were unlike Belize City folks'.

Darius's family immediately took me in as one of their own. Mrs. Martinez, a charismatic and highly respected elder of the community, was fun to be around. I asked her to teach me how to say "Nice to see you," in Garifuna. She said, "Goondatina narehenibu." From then on, when I came to visit, I would first salute her with "Goondatina narehenibu."

54. Stann Creek. Alexandrina Martinez (1903-1997). November 19, 1971.

55. Stann Creek. Tropical Storm Laura during the late afternoon. This picture was taken near Darius Martinez's parents' home while I was visiting during Garifuna Settlement Days. November 21, 1971.

As bad luck would have it, during the weekend of Settlement Days, Stann Creek witnessed the last storm of the 1971 hurricane season. Tropical Storm Laura threatened to come ashore on the evening of Sunday, November 21. Earlier in the day we celebrated as the clouds gathered. Radio Belize broadcasts seemed to indicate that Stann Creek was the target of the storm. That evening, we hunkered down at the Martinez home with the rest of the family. I worried about a tidal surge since the house was only a single-level home built at sea level, barely 300 yards from the ocean.[2] Luckily for us, Laura did a last minute shift to the south, causing agricultural damage to banana crops. However, in Stann Creek, we passed the night nervously, but safely.

Darius and I were up early Monday morning. We had to go to work in Belize City, but found all public transportation was cancelled, and the Hummingbird Highway, our only route to Belmopan and Belize City, was covered with fallen trees.

Chapter 25 gives a brief description of Settlement Days events, which I experienced the following year, 1972.

56. Stann Creek. The Peace Corps couple pictured above arrived from Uganda, following Idi Amin's military coup in January 1971. November 1971.

57. Stann Creek. The circle shows the Martinez family standing in front of their home. The photo was taken from the newly installed telecommunications tower. 1973.

58. Stann Creek. Alexandrina Martinez laughing, her sister-in-law Alphonsa Cassimirro standing on the left, and her sister Abigail Gonzalez.1972.

7
Notes

1 Other communities settled in Belize by the Garifuna during the nineteenth century were: Hopkins, Seine Bight Village, Punta Gorda and Barranco. These villages are located along the southern coast of Belize.

2 Darius Martinez to the author, September 12, 2013. In 1961, Hurricane Hattie, which destroyed 75% of Belize City, also caused devastation in Stann Creek (Dangriga). Most of the damage there was from severe winds. Luckily, the Martinez home was not completely destroyed (Picture 211). Their house was blown off its foundation stilts and held in place by one of the posts that broke through the flooring.

8
National Track and Field Course

From November 3 to December 17, 1971, I taught a nine-session track and field coaches course in Belize City. This course was open to the general public. Students learned how to be better coaches and officials in track and field. Belize City participants included Jaime Sanchez, Juanita Kemp, Bob Moriano, Vernon Vassel, and eight other individuals. They were from different walks of life, including policing, teaching, and business. All had a love of the sport and had found out about the course through the Amateur Athletic Association, public advertising or word of mouth.

Course participants learned the basics of organizing, coaching, and officiating track and field. For each session I handed out information that was compiled into a folder. That way, at the end of the course participants had a fifty-page booklet with all of the information. The previous year, in Sierra Leone, I had taken a similar course that I used as a model. To cover printing costs, we charged a sign-up fee that equaled about twenty-five U.S. cents.

NATIONAL TRACK AND FIELD COURSE
MINISTRY OF LOCAL GOVERNMENT COMMUNITY
AND SOCIAL DEVELOPMENT
BRITISH HONDURAS AMATEUR ATHLETIC ASSOCIATION

The need for a better understanding of the rules governing athletic meetings, and coaching techniques is apparent in British Honduras. A better understanding can mean more interest, and consequently a higher standard of performance. This is essential, if this country is to reach an international level of competition.

You will be given copies of all the material covered in the course. It is suggested that you review all of the information on a topic prior to that session. You should compile these hand-out papers into a resourse file for future reference.

Session number one
> Introduction
> Track size/specifications
> Practical layout

Session number two
> Athletic equipment/care and use
> sprint start tedhnique
> Stop watch/time keeping/judging

Session number three
> Relay racing/ technique/marking/decathlon and pentathlon/middle distance/long distance

Session number four
> Long jump/technique/rules sector layout
> Triple jump/technique/rules/sector layout

Session number five
> Discuss/technique/rules/sector layout
> Shot Put/technique/rules/soctor layout

Session number six
> Study of film loops
> Organization of a sports meeting

Session number seven
> High Jump/technique/rules/sector layout
> Javelin/technique/rules/sector layout

Session number eight
> Hurdles/technique/rules/sector layout
> Pole Vault/technique/rules/sector layout

Session number nine
> Examination

59. Track and Field Course outline 1971-72.

THE MINISTRY OF LOCAL GOVERNMENT, COMMUNITY AND SOCIAL DEVELOPMENT

of

BELIZE

OFFICIALS' AND TRAINERS' TRACK AND FIELD CERTIFICATE

THIS IS TO CERTIFY THAT

MR. JAIME SANCHEZ

has completed an adult course for Coaches and Officials

in Track and Field, held at BELIZE CITY, *From* NOV. 1971 , *To* DEC. 1971

and is recognized by the Ministry in conjunction with the British Honduras

Amateur Athletic Association as worthy of this Certificate of Merit.

DATED JANUARY 1, 1972

Ted W Cox

President B.H.A.A.A.   *Director-Coach, Track and Field.*

60. National Track and Field certificate.

Not thinking there would be any objection, and without first checking with the ministry, I had the country name "Belize" printed on the track and field certificates instead of "British Honduras". In 1971 nobody knew when the official country name change would take place, so my decision raised an eyebrow or two. At least one Belize City participant refused to accept the certificate, suggesting I had let politics enter the course. She pointed out that I was working in cooperation with the British Honduras Amateur Athletic Association, so the certificate should reflect that fact. (The name "Belize" was officially adopted for the country on June 1, 1973.) Since the certificates were already printed, that's how they remained throughout the course, with no further objection that I was aware of.

Ted W. Cox

61. MCC Grounds. Track and Field Course. November 1971.

62. MCC Grounds. Track and Field Course.
Juanita Kemp, second from left, was an officer in
the BHAAA; Jaime Sanchez, second from right,
was a Belize City secondary school teacher; and
Bob Moriano, on the right, was a corporal in the
Belize Special Police Unit. November 1971.

In December, I traveled to the out
districts and Belmopan to make
preparations for conducting a nationwide
track and field clinic. The venues were
arranged primarily at secondary schools
and public recreation areas. My first visit
was to Orange Walk on December 10. There,
I met with Sister Leona, principal of Muffles
College, and Social Development Officer
Dudley Augustine.

63. Orange Walk. Dudley Augustine, Social Development Department, holding a shot. December 10, 1971.

Punta Gorda was the biggest challenge to get to because of its isolation and poor roads. Initial arrangements for a visit there were done through letter.

The out district schedule was as follows:

January 3-16/72	San Ignacio
January 10-24/72	Belmopan
January 27-31/72	Orange Walk
February 1-9/72	Corozal
February 11-26/72	Stann Creek
February 18-23/72	Punta Gorda

By the end of February more than seventy men and women had successfully completed the course throughout the country.

National Track and Field Course Out District Participants 1972		
Raphael L. Cal	San Ignacio	January 15
Lloyd Young	San Ignacio	January 15
Edward Torres	San Ignacio	January 7
David Cruz	San Ignacio	January 4
Earl Morey	San Ignacio	January 4
Adrian Levy	San Ignacio	January 7
Javier Mendez	San Ignacio	January 7
Michael Waight	San Ignacio	January 5
Eugene Cabbinett	San Ignacio	January 4
Jaime Zetina	San Ignacio	January 19
Henry Fandrei	Belmopan	January 10

Othon Castillo	Belmopan	January 10
Evadne Middleton	Belmopan	January 10
George Brown	Belmopan	January 10
Edwin Henderson	Belmopan	January 10
Lois Pitt	Belmopan	January 10
Michael Hyde	Belmopan	January 10
Aloysius Palacio	Belmopan	January 10
Howard Hermans	Belmopan	January 10
Alfredo Gonzalez	Orange Walk	January 21
Ricardo Carballo	Orange Walk	January 21
Solomon Constanza	Orange Walk	January 21
Erasmo Franklin	Orange Walk	January 21
Teresita Blanco	Orange Walk	January 21
Francis Lino	Orange Walk	January 21
Gilda Dennison	Orange Walk	February 1
Richard Quan	Corozal	February 1
Susanne Brabaender	Corozal	February 2
Harold Schmidt	Corozal	February 15
Lorraine Blades	Corozal	February 10
Edgar Gegg	Corozal	February 10
Joan Babb	Corozal	February 10
Inair Marin	Corozal	February 10
Jacinto Flores	Corozal	February 10
Fausto Poot	Corozal	February 10
Victor Lizarraga	Corozal	February 10
Jane Bishop	Corozal	February 10
Joyce Kirk	Corozal	February 10
Benito Cobb	Corozal	February 10
Richard Powell	Corozal	February 9
Antonio Correa	Corozal	February 9
Sylvia Brown	Corozal	February 9
Mary McCarron	Corozal	February 9
Mark Starner	Corozal	February 9
Carl Smith	Stann Creek	February 12
C. Forbes	Stann Creek	February 12

Stanley Castillo	Stann Creek	February 12
Douglas Hypolite	Stann Creek	February 16
Lydia Flores	Stann Creek	February 16
Rudy C. Arana	Stann Creek	February 14
Rodwell N. Leslie	Stann Creek	February 14
Huedney D. Brooks	Stann Creek	February 16
Joseph Castillo	Stann Creek	February 16
David Lewis	Stann Creek	February 16
Alfred Ramirez	Stann Creek	February 16
Anthony Mahuna	Punta Gorda	February 23
George Castro	Punta Gorda	February 23
Luke L. Martinez	Punta Gorda	February 23
Francis Hecker	Punta Gorda	February 23
Franklin Flowers	Punta Gorda	February 23

I was proud that many participants of the track and field course remained actively involved in the sport during my two years of work in Belize.

In January 1972, I also repeated the course in Belize City, but this time as an elective for physical education students at the Belize Teachers' College.

9
Equipment, Athletes, and Preparation

Soon after arrival in country I had made friends with Albert Lovell, a talented woodworking instructor at Junior Secondary School #2 in Belize City. He became a reliable friend who I both worked and socialized with during my stay in Belize.

Ted W. Cox

64. *Belize City. Belize Junior Secondary School #2 woodshop. Albert Lovell, fifth from left. November 3, 1972.*

In October 1971, I discovered that the long jump pit at the MCC Grounds needed upgrading. It was too shallow for safety, only six inches deep instead of the

113

recommended fifteen, and filled with rice husks instead of sand.

From October 10 to 14, Albert constructed a rectangular wooden frame 25' x 9' and the pit was dug to the recommended depth. The frame was then placed so that its top edge was flush with the ground and sand purchased.

Ted W. Cox

65. Belize City. Transferring sand to shore for the long jump pit at MCC Grounds. October 14, 1971.

With a thought to keeping material costs down, I now focused on how track and field equipment could be made locally. In November, Albert constructed a starting block prototype, with adjustable foot placement and costing $2.50 U.S. Eventually he constructed thirty-five starting blocks that were made available to schools and interested athletes (Picture 67).

114

Ted W. Cox

66. *Corozal. Demonstrating measurement technique in the new long jump pit at Fletcher High School. 1972.*

Ted W. Cox

67. *MCC Grounds. Eastern Divisional Secondary School Track Meet. Some athletes were using the starting blocks made by Albert Lovell. March 24, 1973.*

To mark lanes on the field, we usually used non-toxic white powder (calcium carbonate). Without a machine called a dry line marker, you would have to use a bucket and cups to sprinkle the chalk as someone guided you with a tape measure, or follow straight lines guided by stake and string. When I first arrived in Belize we did not have a dry line marker so I ordered some inexpensive markers (Picture 182), thinking they could be attached to a multiple lane extension. This was a poor idea that did not work out.

Then the assistant grounds keeper of the MCC Grounds, Percy Eagan, came forward with a brilliant idea. He thought, why not mix the chalk with water and paint lines on the field? With scraps of wood and a minimum purchase of hardware, Percy proceeded to create a wet marking box and built it right on the field. The machine worked so well that we used it often. He built a new one the following year.

68. MCC Grounds. Track and Field Course. Practicing one way to measure and lay out lanes, with bucket and cups. November 1971.

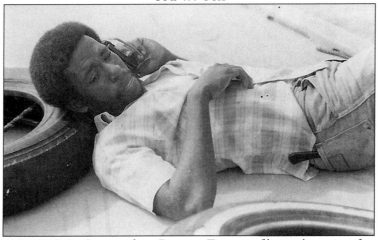

69. MCC Grounds. Percy Eagan listening to the radio. 1971.

70.71.72.
MCC Grounds.
Constructing a wet
marking box. 1971.

73. *MCC Grounds. PCV Chris Dixon demonstrating Percy Eagan's wet marking box. 1972*

Ted W. Cox

74. *Stann Creek. Ned Pitts supervising field marking. 1973.*

Another of my jobs was to seek and develop athletes who could compete at international and Olympic competition levels. In 1971, runner Dorla Flowers had that special potential. The BHAAA considered her a candidate for the upcoming Munich Olympics. At the time Dorla was a high school student at St. Hilda's College in Belize City.

A few months prior to my arrival, Olympic Champion Bill Toomey held a track and field workshop in Belize City. He noticed Dorla's swiftness in the 100M and 200M events. The previous July, Dorla participated at the Central American and Caribbean Games in Jamaica where she gained valuable experience and reached the finals, placing fifth in her event.

I don't remember who introduced me to Dorla, but in November, with the encouragement of Ned Pitts (British Honduras Olympic Committee), I first discussed the possibility of beginning a nine-month training program. The goal was to meet Olympic standards for her events in the 1972 Munich Olympic Games.

75. Belize City. Eastern Divisional Track Meet. Dorla Flowers, third from right. Note the lack of footwear! March 4, 1972.

Contact was made with her mother on November 25, and the principal of her high school, St. Hilda's College, on December 9. The principal approved of a program as long as it did not affect Dorla's schoolwork. The last detail before beginning in earnest was a physical examination. Then in December 1971, with the assistance of James Usher, a nine-month training program was put in place. At first Dorla's workouts went as scheduled, but by March she began losing interest in training. I remember that she wanted to play softball for her school in the spring, and she began to fall short when it came to the track program. Her training schedule was finally dropped. Maybe if my time had been spent coaxing her along and easing up on the discipline, things would have worked out.

When Ned Pitts, president of the British Honduras Olympic Association formally asked me if Dorla would be ready to go to Munich, I informed him that she would not, and that was the official end of her program. A golden opportunity was lost.[1]

Another athlete I enjoyed working with was meteorologist Fred Evans, who developed a passion for the decathlon after attending the same Jamaican track meet with Dorla in 1971. Fred had recently returned from study in Great Britain and was working at the Belize International Airport. His free time became focused on decathlon training. For a time in 1973 we did early morning workouts at the MCC Grounds.

In a 2013 correspondence Fred wrote:

> **Fred:** I used to train with you every morning starting around 6 am. I did running in place followed by 1500 meter work (circuit training). You also worked with me on the shot put and for the pole vault had me "carry" the steel pole the length of the field. I got faster. . .I still use some of what I learned from you to teach/coach my athletes.

Since that time Fred has had a successful career, both as an athlete and coach. In 1974 he became the first Belizean to win first place in an international track event (1500-meter decathlon, Central American and Caribbean Games). He held the Belizean national decathlon record for over twenty years and has been active and highly successful in "Masters" competition since 1999. Fred's athletes have won dozens of awards in Central America and the Caribbean during the past four decades, including his son Alexander, the Central American Octathon champion for two years.

* * * * *

On November 8, 1971, I attended a special meeting at the Belize City Police Station to discuss bringing back the dormant Triangular Track and Field Meet between the British Honduras Amateur Athletic Association, British Army and Belize Police Force.[2] Also attending the

123

meeting were British Honduras Police Inspector Grant, Grenadier Major Gulliver, and Gilmore Hinkson representing the BHAAA. We decided that each team could enter two athletes per event in both running and field competition. We also agreed that the events on the program would include: 100M, 200M, 400M, 800M, 1500M, 5,000M, shot put, discus, javelin, long jump, triple jump, high jump, pole vault, medley relay, and the tug of war. At our next meeting we selected March 11, 1972, for the competition date.

I didn't realize at the time that the Grenadier Battalion was motivated to make this event a showpiece during their deployment in British Honduras. They were keen on track and field and when returning home the following year continued to win various competitions in England. The meet may also have been a clever way to make a statement to Guatemala about the British commitment to Belize.

No matter what the army's motivation might have been, the revival of the track meet was a golden opportunity for Belizean athletes to get fired up and compete against some quality competition. During the following months, a number of open workouts for Belizean athletes were held that eventually led to qualifying trials at the MCC Grounds.

124

During December, Major Gulliver informed me that the garrison was replacing all the foam rubber mattresses at the Airport Camp. At that time the garrison was preparing for the arrival of an additional 360 Grenadiers at the end of January, and new mattresses were part of their preparation. He said the ones in use were old and soiled, but basically in good shape, and offered to give them to the BHAAA for use in the high jump and pole vault. We accepted the offer and within four weeks were in possession of over 200 mattresses.

At the end of December, I gave Lieutenant Bob G. Woodfield, the garrison administrative officer, an inventory of equipment the BHAAA possessed. There weren't many items: one 16-pound shot, one senior discus, three stopwatches and an improvised high jump standard. I informed Lieutenant Woodfield that I planned to construct a shot put pad, a pole vault and high jump area, as well as having already upgraded the long jump pit at the MCC Grounds.

On January 11, I was told that the garrison had pole vault standards, high jump standards, cross bars and pole vault poles that we could use.

One of my job objectives was to make contact with athletic firms in the United States from which the ministry could order a moderate amount of athletic equipment. During a conversation with Major Gulliver, he suggested that we order the equipment through the Airport Camp NAAFI Store (Navy, Army and Air Force Institute, similar to the American PX). The prices would be wholesale and the equipment delivered to the Airport Camp. This was a great opportunity to save money for the ministry. On January 14, Major Gulliver agreed to have Lieutenant Woodfield order four discuses, four javelins, three shot puts, two pole vault poles, four cross bars, one pole vault standard, one high jump standard, one dozen batons, three stop watches and a 200-foot measuring tape. Prior to ordering, Lieutenant Woodfield sent a cost estimate to the Ministry of Local Government for approval.

I soon met Sergeant Dick Slater, who was assigned to work with me on this event. He immediately became a friend and a big help preparing for the Triangular Track and Field Meet.

76. Corozal. James Usher, BHAAA, and Sgt. Dick Slater, Grenadier Guards, discuss the upcoming Triangular Track and Field Meet on June 11, 1972, over Belikan Beer (a popular local brew). April 1972.

Dick jumped into the Belize City social scene, and soon dated a pretty Creole girl with an attractive mane of red hair. She managed a bar on Albert Street near Bird's Isle. Dick ended up volunteering many off-duty hours there serving drinks, and keeping order.

During planning of the Triangular Track and Field Meet, I was informed that the army wanted to do the layout of the track at MCC Grounds. As far as I was concerned, this was good news. I would be able to focus on the overall program and coach athletes without worrying about layout details. Copies were made of all related information and handed over to Lieutenant Woodfield.

On Sunday, March 5, a qualifying track and field meet for the BHAAA was held to select Belizean athletes. Officials of the association had advertised the tryouts and participants came forward. During the previous few months I had scheduled various track workouts and individuals had been working on their own, so we had a good group of competitors.

When March 11 arrived, two days of rain caused the track meet to be postponed until March 22. The army, for whatever reason, had to reschedule the March 22 date at the last minute. Not to be discouraged, the BHAAA used March 22 to good advantage. The athletic field was already prepared, allowing us to hold qualifying trials in the 200- 400- and 800-meter races.

On Thursday, April 6, I met with representatives at the Front Street Magistrate Building in Belize City (from the Grenadier Guards, Major John O'Connel; Belize Police, Jorge Palacio; and the BHAAA, Gilmore Hinkson, James Usher, and Norrin O. Meighan).

We set June 11 as the new date for the Triangular Track and Field Meet.

9
Notes

[1] January 1972 was an exciting time for the British Honduras Olympic Committee. People were looking forward to the upcoming Olympics in Munich. Ned Pitts told me that the annual general meeting on January 10 was the most successful he could remember with over 30 individuals present. Among those attending were:

President of British Honduras Olympic Association, Ned Pitts
President of Boxing, Mr. and Mrs. Gilbert Ellis
President of Cycling, Mr. and Mrs. Phillip Rosado
President of Basketball, Mr. Michael Usher
President of Football, Mr. and Mrs. Jorge Pelayo
President of Weight Lifting, Mr. and Mrs. Nestor Vasquez
President of Softball, Mr. and Mrs. Leslie Isaacs
President of A.A.A., Mr. and Mrs. Norrin Meighan
President of Tennis, Mr. and Mrs. Joseph Fuller.

[2] A number of pictures that were taken at the 1972 Triangular Track and Field Meet are included in Chapter 19.

10
Regional and National Track and Field Competitions, 1972

THE AMATEUR ATHLETIC ASSOCIATION

Mrs. Juanita Kemp
— 1st. vice president

Mr. Anthony Christie
— 2nd. vice president

Mr. Gilmore Hinkson
— treasurer

Mr. Ted Cox
— coach (peace corps)

Mr. Richard Coye
— ex-officio member

Mr. James Usher
— asst. secretary

Page 27.

77. Belize City. National Secondary School Track and Field program. April 22, 1972.

131

From the time of my arrival in the country, Belizeans expressed the desire to organize a national track and field competition for secondary schools. Following a discussion with Ned Pitts and other individuals about this idea, members of the BHAAA formed a committee and planning began. Meetings were held with interested secondary school principals and dates were set.

The country was divided into sections, each to conduct divisional track and field meets, with the best athletes coming to Belize City for the national track meet scheduled for April 22, 1972.

The inter-school competition schedule was laid out as follows:

March 4, 1972	Belize City schools
March 24, 1972	Belmopan/San Ignacio
April 14, 1972	Corozal/Orange Walk
April 15, 1972	Stann Creek
April 22, 1972	Belize City National Secondary School Track and Field Meet

78. MCC Grounds. Eastern Divisional Track Meet. High jump. March 4, 1972.

79. MCC Grounds. Eastern Divisional Track Meet. 100-meter race. March 4, 1972.

80. MCC Grounds. Eastern Divisional Track Meet. Distance race. March 4, 1972.

Letter Home
March 5, 1972
Belize City

      Yesterday was the Belize City Secondary School Divisional Track Meet. It was a big success and a lot of spectators came to see the track meet. I was also involved in a track meet today (Sunday), the Triangular Track and Field Meet eliminations for the Amateur Athletic Association.

81.   Stann   Creek.   Southern
Divisional Track Meet program.
April 15, 1972.

MESSAGE FROM THE PRESIDENT B.H.A.A.A.

Mr. Norrin O. Meighan

It is a great honour for me to extend greetings and best wishes to the organizers and participants in the Southern Districts Track and Field Meet.

I am sure that the athletes shall be giving of their best to win and to take part well.

May you have a successful Meet and may the better athlete win.

82. Stann Creek. Southern Divisional Track Meet program. April 15, 1972.

Letter Home
April 18, 1972
Belize City

Dear Mother,
    The National Secondary School Track and Field Meet will be held this weekend. Then I'll have a little slack in my work. Last week I drove the Peace Corps pickup truck to Corozal to assist with the Northern Divisional Track and Field Meet. After lunch I drove over the Mexican border into Chetumal (about ten miles). I was traveling with two friends, one British soldier and a Belizean.
    I received a letter from Peter Deloes in Sierra Leone. He says he'll be going to Nova Scotia for an eight-month Social Development Course. Many people from British Honduras have also gone to this place.
    So that's the latest. Waiting your reply.
Love, Teddy

Richard Coye, member of the BHAAA, wrote the following historical comment that appeared in the official program of the National Secondary School Track and Field Meet on April 22, 1972, held at the MCC Grounds:

    The British Honduras Amateur Athletic Association was founded in 1956.
    Only one year after its birth, our Association sent a track team to Jamaica to compete in the British West Indian Games, today known as The Central American and Caribbean Games. Those representing our country were S.F. Smith, Ned Pitts

and Roy Burgess. Roy Burgess was successful in the high jump event, clearing a height of 6'4.

Three years later, a second team traveled to Jamacia for a similar event and this time a female contender, Miss Roacke, was named among the competitors.

In 1962 two athletes, Leroy Lucas and Eustace Gill, accompanied by a delegate and a coach, traveled to Perth, Australia, to participate in the British and Commonwealth Games at the invitation of the Australian Association. However, the Association at home was not asleep. Realizing that the athletes for tomorrow would grow from the youth in the schools, they planned and successfully carried through the First Inter-Secondary Track and Field Meet (Belize City Schools), which is now an annual event.

In the years between 1966 and 1969 the Association went through somewhat of a decline. In 1967 we were again invited but we were unable to attend due to financial reasons.

In 1968 the Olympic Games were held in Mexico and only two of our athletes attended. Only one of the athletes was able to compete in all scheduled races. In July 1971, new potential was shown in the person of Dorla Flowers, who along with three male athletes, traveled to the Caribbean Games, where she reached the finals and placed fifth in her race.

Meanwhile, at home, the Association has held meets at least twice a year and has worked overtime to keep the interest in athletics afloat. This current year shows much promise.

The dormant Triangular Meet will again take place this year. Not only will there be a local inter-secondary school meet, but the Association is spreading its wings to correct a long overdue oversight. In April of this year, there will be a National Secondary School Meet in which schools from all over the country will be participating.

Both the country and the Association realize that we have the potential. We only lack the know-how. We are trying to correct this. In doing so, we can boast a qualified coach in the person of Mr. Ted W. Cox who has already done much improvement in the first eight months of his two-year stay.

In closing, the present officials of the Association would like to thank those people who have stuck with the Association through thick and thin. Without them every year would seem like a beginning.

Journal
April 22, 1972
Belize City

Today was the first National Secondary School Track and Field Meet held at the MCC Grounds in Belize City. It was a big success.

Ted W. Cox

83. MCC Grounds. Grenadier Dick Slater, starter, and Juanita Kemp, holding the card, at the National Secondary School Track Meet. April 22, 1972.

Ted W. Cox

84. MCC Grounds. National Secondary School Track Meet. April 22, 1972.

140

85. MCC Grounds. National Secondary School Track Meet. E. Morris from Wesley College wins the 100-meter dash. April 22, 1972.

11
Danger from the Border

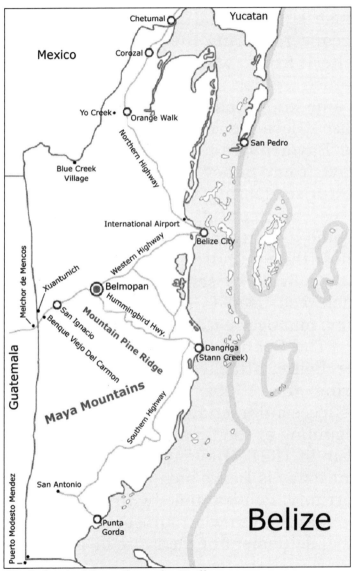

E. Selected locations in Belize

From a historical perspective, the Spanish never physically occupied the territory today known as Belize. Following the collapse of the Mayan Empire only British subjects had arrived, beginning with buccaneers during the 1600s. They wanted shelter from which they could attack Spanish ships. Eventually, these men became known as Baymen, in recognition of Belize's location in the Bay of Honduras. The Baymen gradually turned their efforts away from piracy and focused on legal enterprise. During the 1700s they brought slaves to harvest timber, and forestry became the mainstay of the economy for almost three hundred years. At first Baymen made a living by selling logwood, the sap of which was used to dye clothes in Europe.[1] Later, mahogany was the main export.

The Spanish, who claimed sovereignty over Belize, attacked the settlers repeatedly during the 1700s. Ultimately, they were unsuccessful in ending British occupation. Beginning at the time of independence from Spain in 1821, Guatemala regarded the area that today is Belize as a rogue piece of their territory. Political talks with Great Britain resulted in what appeared to be a settlement of the issue in 1859.

86. *Belize City. Squaring mahogany for export.
Late 1920s.*[2]

In 1862, Belize became the colony of British Honduras. Seventy years later, during the 1930s, Guatemala renewed agitation on the claim to British Honduras. The fact that oil had been discovered in Mexico and Venezuela may have influenced this attention. In 1940, Guatemala declared that the 1859 treaty was void because Britain failed to build an access road from its border through British Honduras to the Caribbean coast as agreed upon in the 1859 treaty. Then, in 1945, Guatemala adopted a new constitution that included British Honduras (Belicé), as a province within its

145

border. Guatemalan threats of aggression in 1948 prompted the formation of a permanent British garrison for defense of the colony. In March, the first troops to arrive were from the 1st Battalion Gloucestershire.

87. *British Honduras. Woodcutter preparing to fell a mahogany tree. Late 1920s.*[3]

Beginning in the 1950s, Britain started gradual passage of colonial control to the Belizeans amidst continued Guatemalan hostility.

When I arrived in August 1971, the resident garrison consisted of one company of 180 Scots Guards who were about to be relieved by an equal number of Grenadier Guardsmen. There was also a small staff of eight officers who maintained and administered the military infrastructure, which included a stores officer, medical officer, signals officer, local intelligence officer and a REME (Royal Electrical and Mechanical Engineers) warrant officer responsible for transport.

The main military base was located at the Airport Camp a few miles from Belize City. The mission of the troops was to hold the airport in case of a Guatemalan invasion until reinforcements could be flown in. They were also to secure the national border through constant reconnaissance and to practice crisis scenarios. Secondary missions included giving assistance to civil authorities during emergencies and providing training to the local volunteer guard.

In September 1971, a secret eighteen-page report from the Ministry of Defense in England was distributed to colonial authorities. The report predicted that the garrison would not survive a Guatemalan invasion for more than a few hours. This account came as no surprise to those allowed to read it.

At the time, Guatemalan armed forces were about ten thousand strong of whom only a few hundred were highly trained. A core of 300 skilled paratroopers, schooled by U.S. forces in Panama, was experienced in jungle fighting and fiercely loyal to their president. The Guatemalan air force was small, but well qualified compared to other Central American countries. F-51 Mustang fighters equipped with napalm and 50-caliber guns could provide air cover. There were also eight brand new Cessna A-37B Dragon Flies. The Dragon Flies were a popular and effective ground attack jet used by Americans in Vietnam.

British defenses, on the other hand, were not prepared for a lightning invasion. Their strategy was that through intense reconnaissance at the border, they could initiate the arrival of reinforcements from Britain within four days. There was no radar or air power to support the 180 infantry ground troops if overrun before that time.

The secret report recommended reinforcement of the garrison commencing in February 1972.[4]

88. Belmopan. 1st Battalion Devon and Dorset Regiment gives a demonstration at the National Agricultural Show. November 12, 1972.

11
Notes

[1] Today, the dye produced from logwood, also called bloodwood, is used as a stain for microscopic slides.

[2] John Everitt, "The Growth and Development of Belize City," *Belizean Studies,* (Volume 14, No. 1), 1986. Colonial Governor Sir Eric Swayne (1906-1913) wrote in 1917 that at one time mahogany logs were rafted down to Belize and squared on undeveloped areas of the city (Picture 86). The wood chips that resulted from the squaring sank along with whiskey bottles and log ends into the mud and helped build a base on which parts of Belize City were later developed.

[3] During the first half of the twentieth century mahogany was the colony's main export and chicle was second (a natural gum traditionally used in making chewing gum). In 1945, forest products made up 90% of the country's total exports. By the 1970s it was down to 2%.

[4] Rowland White, *Phoenix Squadron* (U.K.: Transworld Publishers, 2009). Most of the military information for this chapter was found in White's book.

12
Governor
Sir Richard Posnett

In 1964, British Honduras began local self-government rule, an important transition leading to eventual independence. At the time, the same status was enjoyed by six other Caribbean nations: St. Lucia, St. Kitts, St Vincent, Grenada, Dominica and Antigua.[1]

In 1972, Sir Richard Posnett was appointed the twentieth governor of the colony, a position he held during the next four years.[2] The governor of a British colony was the queen's representative and leader in external affairs, defense, and civil service.

Posnett was born in India in 1919 to British missionaries. When seven years old he began his formal education in England. In 1941, during World War II, he began colonial service as a district officer in Uganda. There he worked for twenty-three years. During 1962 he was entrusted with Ugandan independence celebrations with a budget of over 500 thousand U.S. dollars.

Letter Home
June 9, 1972
Belize City

Dear Mother,
    On Monday I received word from the Ministry of Social Development that the governor of the colony, Sir Richard Posnett, wanted to meet with Mr. Hinkson and myself. So Wednesday morning we went to Belmopan and saw him for about 90 minutes. A very friendly man and keenly interested in sports. He wondered why a country like this does not have a first class track for athletics. He said he would be willing to assist in such a project if Mr. Hinkson and I would get a self-help fundraising committee of interested citizens organized.[3]
    About this summer. I will be coming up in July for sure. I wrote to Smithford Products about some part-time work and they replied that I would have a job. I believe that this is against Peace Corps policy, but I will need some money to buy clothes and pay for my bus fare back to Belize. I plan to leave July 1st via bus for Mexico City. If all goes well I will be in Tijuana by July 3 or 4th. I'll catch a bus up to Ontario from San Diego and would like to stay until the end of July.
It's your son, Love Ted

Posnett's interest in track and field went back to his school days in England where he was an accomplished hurdler.

In 1954, while serving as colonial administrator in Uganda, Posnett got involved with the local amateur athletic association. He was instrumental in

152

organizing and qualifying Ugandan athletes for the British Empire and Commonwealth Games held in Vancouver, Canada, that year.

Rob Thurston

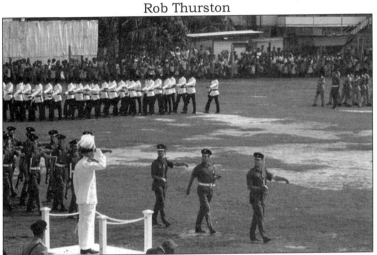

89. MCC Grounds. Governor Posnett salutes the troops at the Queen's Birthday Parade. 1973.

The Queen's Birthday Parade, held at the MCC Grounds, was the biggest parade of the year in British Honduras. Officially called the Commonwealth Holiday in 1966, the event was celebrated around May 24 each year. Members of the British Forces, Volunteer Guard, Police Special Force, Fire Service, Ex-Serviceman's League, Boy Scouts and just about anyone wearing a uniform was involved. This was the one day each year that the governor dressed up in his official colonial uniform, complete with feathered hat.

90. *Belize City. Standing in review at Memorial Park, from left to right, Premier George Price, Governor Richard Posnett and Prince Philip during His Royal Highness's state visit. 1975.*

12
Notes

[1] Richard Posnett, *The Scent of Eucalyptus* (London: The Radcliffe Press, 2001).

[2] Prior to 1884, British Honduras had a string of seven lieutenant governors that were subordinate to the governor in Jamaica.

[3] In one follow-up to this meeting, I met with Les Hall from the public works department that September. He advised that it would cost about $40,000 B.H. to sufficiently fill the center field at the National Stadium by dredge.

13
On War and Peace

On January 17, 1972, intelligence received by the British Foreign Office in England indicated that Guatemala was about to invade British Honduras. Over the following week, the governments of Nicaragua, Honduras and Mexico all concurred that an invasion was at hand. The resident Grenadier Guards were put on alert and began preparing for war. They were only 180 strong, with no radar or air support. They knew an attack at that moment would be devastating.[1]

I was focused on my job, unaware like the rest of the population of the imminent danger.

Nine days later, on January 26, I was working in Orange Walk when Sir Richard Posnett, the new governor of the colony, flew from Jamaica on a commercial flight to assume his post. During the trip, he showed the pilot an official telegram stating that an invasion of British Honduras by Guatemala was feared. He requested the captain confirm that things were normal in Belize before landing: "Just make sure that the British are in control of the airfield before you land. If there's any doubt, stay clear."[2]

Later that same day, reinforcements of the 2nd Battalion Grenadier Guards began arriving from England. Two days later the British aircraft carrier *Ark Royal*, which was in the North Atlantic and steaming towards the Caribbean, launched an impressive long-range flyover of Belize City by two of its Buccaneer jets. This was done to demonstrate Britain's resolve to defend the colony.

Ted W. Cox

91. Blue Creek, a large Mennonite farming village in northern British Honduras, looking towards La Union, Mexico. If the Guatemalans invaded while the garrison was undermanned, and the airport fell as expected, the Blue Creek area in northern British Honduras was considered a safe dropping zone for reinforcement troops and supplies from England. September 10, 1972.

By January 30, the resident garrison had increased to at least 540 strong, and the anticipated invasion did not occur.

158

Sometime after this initial influx of British military, Grenadier Dick Slater told me something worded like: "Let the bloody Guats come, Ted. They'll be stopped at Teakettle."[3]

In 1975, plans were uncovered in Guatemala that revealed how determined and tricky the Guatemalans had been. The suggestion was made from Rowland White's research that the big prize eyed was not Belmopan, the international airport or Belize City, but to the south in the Toledo District. This area was isolated, underdeveloped and defenseless in January 1972.[4] Their strategy was straightforward and could have been carried out swiftly. All that stood between Guatemalan occupation and the whole of southern British Honduras in mid-January 1972 was a small police station manned by one officer in Punta Gorda, the southern district community of 2,100. We may never know for sure why they didn't invade.

Starting in late January 1972, and for the next fifteen years, British regimental numbers in Belize increased, as did support units. These included the Royal Corps of Signals, Royal Corps of Engineers, the Royal Electrical and Mechanical Engineers, and units attached to the Royal Air Force who took care of radar. The air force also looked after Bofors antiaircraft cannon, later

159

replaced by Rapier antiaircraft missile installations. Harrier jets were introduced in 1975.[5]

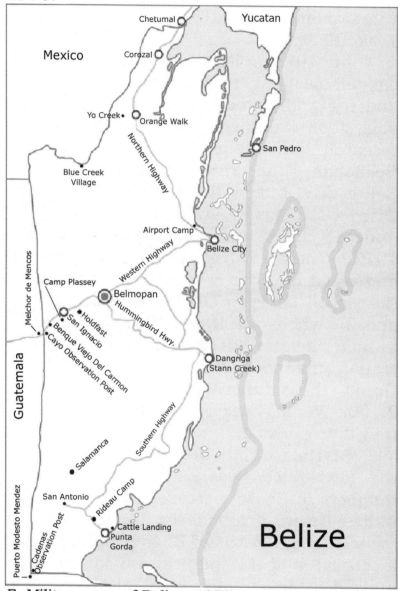

F. Military map of Belize, 1975

In 1975, over 1,500 British military were stationed in Belize, with infantry positioned in six permanent camps and various observation posts:

1. Airport Camp (Price Barracks), near Belize City, was located adjacent to the International Airport. British Force Headquarters, the RAF detachments (Harrier jets, Puma support utility helicopters, Rapier air defense).

2. Holdfast Camp (Belizario) was situated near San Ignacio. The camp's manifesto included forward jungle patrolling and manning observation posts (OP). At the Cayo OP troops watched the cross border approaches from the Guatemalan town Ciudad Melchor de Mencos.

3. Plassey Camp, also located near San Ignacio in the Cayo District, was smaller than Holdfast. Plassey supported reconnaissance platoons along with mortar and anti-tank platoons.

4. Cattle Landing Camp was located on the coast north of Punta Gorda. This post monitored sea approaches.

5. Salamanca Camp in the Toledo District had duties including forward jungle patrol near Pueblo Viejo and manning the Cadenas observation post. The OP was located above the Guatemalan town of Puerto Modesto Mendez on the other side of the Sarstoon River.

6. Rideau Camp (Camp Fairweather) was about three miles from Punta Gorda and was the largest camp in the southern district. It included elements of Royal Engineers and Royal Artillery. There was also an infantry company whose main task was patrolling some of the most remote rainforest areas in the Toledo District.[6]

92. Cayo. Camp Holdfast (Belizario) was the first support camp built in response to the Guatemalan threat of 1972. About 140 soldiers were stationed there when I visited in April 1973.

93.Toledo District. A Puma helicopter sits perched next to the Cadenas Observation Post across the Sarstoon River from the Guatemalan town of Puerto Modesto Mendez.

94. Cayo Observation Post, originally established in 1972, overlooks Melchor de Mencos, Guatemala. 1986.

Royal Irish Regiment Museum

95. Toledo District. Salamanca Camp.

Prior to 1972, Guatemala had been intimidating Belize with at least one unanswered reconnaissance flight over Belize City and paratroop drop exercises along the border. By rolling the dice and invading at the right time, Guatemalan leaders could have taken the south of British Honduras through a straightforward occupation. In that scenario, considering the anti-colonial demeanor at the United Nations in 1972, Guatemala would probably have had international sympathy, at least officially, from surrounding countries for out-maneuvering a major world power. Then, the question in Britain would have been whether to negotiate with the Guatemalans over the southern real estate, or go in and take it back. Those in favor of taking the land back would say that Guatemala was neocolonial in its ambitions and not entitled to any part of British Honduras.

However, by February 1972, the arrival of British reinforcements rapidly regained the military upper hand. The window of opportunity for a successful, rapid, and probably bloodless military occupation by Guatemala had passed after those closing days of January 1972.

When yet another crisis flared up in 1975, newly arrived British Harrier jets would fly up to the border and very impressively hover, turn around, then blast out of the area. British Gurka units (Nepalese), were also parachuted into the Mountain Pine Ridge (Map E, Page 143). This tactic sent a chilling message across the border.

13
Notes

[1] Posnett, Richard, *The Scent of Eucalyptus* (London: The Radcliffe Press, 2001).

[2] Rowland White, *Phoenix Squadron* (London: Transworld Publishers, 2009), 230.

[3] Teakettle is located just west of Belmopan. At that location is a natural narrowing along the Western Highway where anti-tank defenses could be set up to advantage.

[4] White, 239.

[5] Dave Anderson, telephone interview by the author, June 21, 2013.

[6] This information was adapted from The Royal Irish web page: www.Royal-Irish.com

14
Isolated in Punta Gorda

In 1972 the road to Punta Gorda from Belmopan was closed 40% of the year due to high river water and low-built plank bridges. Most of the 160 inches of annual rainfall in the south occurred from May to November.

Ted W. Cox

96. Southern Highway to Punta Gorda. During the rainy season, this crossing, like many along the Southern Highway, was covered by the rising river, making travel by road impossible. February 18, 1972.

As the rainy season got seriously underway in June 1972, Associate Peace

Corps Director Rob Thurston drove two Volunteers to their posting in Punta Gorda. At the time, river waters all along the Southern Highway had begun to rise. While crossing one of the plank bridges, Rob paused long enough to take the dramatic picture seen below. In the photo, PCV Bill Kolberg and PCV Kim Kennedy guide the way across the bridge by carefully walking along the wheel planks. After they reached Punta Gorda, the river continued to rise. Within two days most bridges along the Southern Highway were under water and stayed that way for the next five months. Rob flew back to Belize City, leaving the vehicle stranded.

Rob Thurston

97. Southern Highway. The start of the rainy season swamps the plank bridge near Punta Gorda. PCV Bill Kolberg and PCV Kim Kennedy guide the way. The bridge remained under water for about five months. June 1972.

A few months prior to Rob's daring trip, I made the same journey to conduct a scheduled track and field clinic in Punta Gorda for a week. The road and bridges were dry at the time (Picture 96).

Journal
February 18, 1972 – Friday
Punta Gorda

National Track and Field Clinic.
Left Belize City at 6:00 a.m. for Punta Gorda in Ministry of Local Government vehicle. I will spend a week in Punta Gorda teaching the Track and Field Coaches Clinic. By 4:30 p.m. I was in Punta Gorda at the Civic Center where Social Development Officer Mr. Franklin Flowers had arranged a meeting with people interested in taking the course. I explained how the classes would be taught and scheduled the first session for tomorrow at the town football field at 4:30 p.m. Those signed up are:
1.Anthony Mahuna
2.George Castro
3.Luke L. Martinez
4.Francis Hecker-Marketing Board
5.Franklin Flowers-Social Dev. Officer

Journal
Punta Gorda
February 21, 1972 – Monday
    Met at football field at 4:30 p.m. for Session #4, Long Jump and Triple Jump. All went well.
    That evening I met an Englishman working as an advisor in the Public Works Department. He spent thirteen years in Brazil and seven in Uganda.

He said that he was involved in commandeering vehicles for the military coup in Uganda when Idi Amin took control of the country. He said that he was in charge of Government vehicles. We had an interesting conversation about the Portuguese and their influence on Africa.

Journal
February 22, 1972 – Tuesday
Punta Gorda

Francis Hecker took me to three primary schools located outside of Punta Gorda to deliver circulars regarding a field day to be held in Punta Gorda on March 9. Saddleback Elementary (a Catholic school), Fairview, and a Methodist school. Most of the students at Fairview and the Methodist schools were of East Indian heritage.

The headmaster of Saddleback said some of the students were Jehovah Witnesses and that their parents would not let them participate in any sport.

We also visited San Antonio Village and I saw Leon Panning, a PCV that I trained with in Puerto Rico, and a PCV named Kent Keller. Kent and his family are going back to the U.S. instead of staying for a third year because of baby care difficulties.

Journal
Punta Gorda
February 23, 1972 – Wednesday

I received a telegram from the ministry informing that a transport would come on Friday to pick me up. I will be going to Stann Creek, a four-hour drive from Punta Gorda.

98. Near Punta Gorda. Fairview Elementary School. February 22, 1972.

Journal
February 27, 1972
Belize City

Word is out that the federal budget for funding the Peace Corps was cut to $72 million dollars. We don't know yet what effect, if any, this will have for Peace Corps, British Honduras.

173

15
Glimpses of Peace Corps Life

Richard Nixon was not a big fan of the Peace Corps, John Kennedy's inspiration. In early 1972, while Nixon was President, there were rumors in Washington, D.C., that Congress might cut Peace Corps funding. I first heard of this possibility at the Peace Corps Office in Belize City. Right away, I bet PCV Tarmo Jaagus a case of beer that we would not have to leave - even if a cut occurred. My fingers were crossed. By March, to our relief, word was out that we would stay.

During my first year in Belize I rented an apartment with fellow PCV Neal Hammond. The house was located on Baymen Avenue, on the north side of Belize City. During a telephone conversation on September 11, 2012, we reminded ourselves how bad we were at keeping house as bachelors:

Neal: I remember the time we poisoned the cockroaches. It was one of those bait type cockroach repellants. It was probably illegal in the States. You sprinkled that stuff on the floor in the kitchen. We had already seen some of the cockroaches coming out. So you sprinkled this stuff on the floor. Several hundred cockroaches came out and died that night. I think you got the job of sweeping them up.

Ted: I do remember that. We could hear them during the night as they were in the agony of death. Yes, I remember those cockroach egg pods along the corners of the doors and windows. I looked at those pods but didn't realize what they were until we dealt with the problem. Boy, we were sure knuckleheads.

Neal was very sensitive to cold showers, and our shower water was definitely cold because it came from the outdoor cistern some distance from the house. The water flow was slow due to gravity feed, and the pipe held only a limited volume of water. I got the idea to paint the pipes black and this did the trick for Neal. The rainwater in the pipes absorbed more solar heat, so he could take a short shower that was at least not so uncomfortable.

As a Volunteer, Neal did remarkable work for three years in Belize. He was a nutritionist, and his job was everything that had to do with food.

Neal: I was part of a food and nutritional committee. These were people from the Ministry of Health, Share, Ministry of Agriculture, and Ministry of Education. We would meet monthly to evaluate and do studies on the population. It was interesting because they had contacts with the World Health Organization with Incap. The rice and bean production was a big part of that committee.

There was not much food production in Belize in 1971. That's how I found out that the Bevis Ranch was producing rice and beans, and the consumption of rice and beans was part of the nutritional study that we were doing. So that's how I wound up meeting with them. I traveled around to weigh and take the height of all the children in the country entering the first grade. About 3,500 children. We had to go into some really remote villages. That was a Belizean study. C.A.R.E. provided the transportation. The Ministry of Health took care of the people. Usually, that was an aid worker (somebody to take down the notes, count the children, liaison with the school), and myself, who went to these communities. The job was easy in Belize City because everybody was there, but out in the places like Sales Si Puedes, or Maypen, some of those places you had to pack in for a couple of hours.

Ted: What were they going to use that study for?

Neal: The government wanted to determine the level of malnutrition in the country.

When I first arrived the chief medical officer for the country was a Scotsman. He told me outright that there was no malnutrition in the country. As soon as he retired, a young Belizean guy took his place, who was all for trying to find out the real situation.

We found out that there really was a lot of malnutrition. There was a pretty high percentage of the kids who were malnourished. Even though people would say these are big strong people of African descent, we found some really malnourished children. Mayans, Mestizos, Caribs, Creole, it was across the board.

I stayed for a third year and still have my data sheet from the survey I made throughout the country of six-year-olds. The smallest kid that was measured in the country weighed twenty-two pounds. He was not sick. He was healthy and running around. I believe that malnourishment stunted his growth. Especially out in the country there were about 75% malnourished. First, second or third degree malnutrition. We didn't count the ones that died or did not make it to first grade. The infant mortality in Belize was just about the same as it was in Guatemala and Honduras. Probably 25% of the children died in the first five years. For example, here in the States mortality would be something like two per hundred thousand. In Belize it would be thousands per hundred thousand.

After studying the results of the survey, Neal found that the four top schools with healthy children in the country were St. Catherine Primary School and Mrs. Yorke's Infant School in Belize City, plus one primary school in Corozal and one infant school in Stann Creek. All four institutions catered to children from more affluent families.

In 1964, American Albert L. Bevis and his son Chuck leased 11,000 acres of land in the Mountain Pine Ridge at Big Falls. There they developed a mechanized farming and ranching operation to raise rice and beans for the local and export market. In 1971 the Bevis operation harvested over 10 million pounds of rice.[1]

In May of 1973, Neal and I borrowed the Peace Corps truck and went to the Bevis Ranch to purchase rice and bran for his project with the Ministry of Health.

99. Mountain Pine Ridge. PVC Neal Hammond loading sacks of bran and broken rice onto the Peace Corps truck at Bevis Ranch mill. May 1973.

The Belize government wanted to improve nutrition by fostering homegrown chicken production, particularly in the south of the country. An obstacle to local production of chickens was the high cost of imported chicken feed. Neal was asked to make chicken feed from local sources to help lower the feed costs to the farmers, and the Bevis Ranch was able to supply a needed component.

Neal: One of the things I was doing with the rice bran was making chicken feed. We got a grant from the Inter-American Foundation, which was funded by the U.S. Congress. They funded small projects. There were a number of small co-ops that were starting to raise chickens. At that time they had to import all of their chicken feed from Guatemala and other countries. So I made an indigenous feed that was made of all local ingredients. We did add some sesame seed from Mexico, but it was a small amount. Mainly it was rice bran, which was broken rice and meat meal from the Bevis Ranch. The bran is the outer portion of the brown rice removed when the rice is processed into white rice. The meat meal came from the meat packing plant in Belize City. At the plant they sold a product called 'meat meal', which was cooked, ground leftovers. We put the meal into the chicken feed mix to raise the protein level. There was molasses from the sugar mill and sesame meal from a border town in Mexico. We also added some imported vitamins and minerals. Test batches of feed were fed to chicks and laying hens to determine the feed efficiency before selling the feed to family chicken raisers.

100. PCV Neal Hammond fitting the vertical mixing machine that he used to make test batches of chicken feed. 1973.

In 1972, the Mennonite community of Spanish Lookout had a store, located at the corner of Pickstock and North Front Street in Belize City. There they sold furniture, poultry, vegetables, meat, milk and cheese. More than once I prepared fried chicken from their fryers. Sometimes when working at the MCC Grounds I went home for lunch. On those days I stopped at the tortilla factory near St. Joseph's Church to get fresh tortillas to toast on my skillet, along with top quality Mennonite cheddar cheese.[2]

* * * * *

One of the more unusual Peace Corps Volunteer jobs was that of speleologists PCV Barbara MacLeod and PCV Dave Albert. They were originally assigned to the Belize Archeology Department to map the country's underground rivers formed by the erosion of limestone from flowing water over the centuries. Assessing Mayan ceremonial use of the numerous limestone caves soon became part of their assignment. I accompanied them on two of their first outings.

The work of these Volunteers was hazardous. The job required special skills to avoid getting hopelessly lost in the maze of unexplored caverns. I learned that lesson on the first of two explorations with Barbara

183

and Dave. While they moved ahead of me deep into the cave complex, I went through a narrow opening that revealed a new cavern. A sense of fear came over me as I realized how easy it would be to get disoriented in the hollowed out subterranean world.

Letter Home
September 20, 1971
Belize City

Last Friday I went to Belmopan (new capital of the country). Two volunteers, who are cavers (spelunkers), took me to St. Herman's Cave, and we went spelunking for six hours. One of them, named Barbara MacLeod, lent me a hard hat complete with a carbide lamp. This was my only light supply as we went about 2,000 feet, winding around inside of the cave. Big stalagmites and stalactites were around us. At one point numerous bats in a narrow passage overran us. The bats came flying straight at me, and then veered off inches from my body. A few minutes later I bent over to drink some water from a stream we were in and accidentally extinguished my carbide light. All was pitch black. I called ahead to Barbara to come back and help me.

We found some old Mayan pottery, probably 1,300 years old. This was a very neat adventure. Belize is loaded with caves.

It's me, Teddy

101. PCV Barbara MacLeod taking notes from villagers on the Mayan language during spelunking trip. 1971.

Letter Home
May 3, 1972
Belize City

Dear Mother and Family,

I was invited to go on another spelunking trip near Cave Branch with Peace Corps Volunteer spelunkers Barbara MacLeod and Dave Albert. We parked by a scruffy cocoa plantation next to the Southern Highway and were led through the jungle by Belizean guide Buck Cox. We all had machetes to hack our way through the jungle for about 90 minutes. At one point Buck seemed a bit lost. We finally reached a large limestone sinkhole crater, where we rappelled down about 50 feet. Off to one side was the entrance to Petroglyph Cave complex. There appeared to be some kind of natural altar used by the Mayans at the entrance. Inside the cave we found a human skeleton and some other artifacts. Near the entrance I found a vase that had been set in that spot at least 900 years earlier. It was cemented in place by centuries of water minerals solidifying at its base.

102. Cave Branch. Guide Buck Cox rappels down the sinkhole at Petroglyph Cave while PCV Barbara MacLeod looks on. May 3, 1972.

103. Cave Branch. PCV Dave Albert, PCV Barbara MacLeod and guide Buck Cox sitting at the entrance to Petroglyph Cave. The pottery, found near the cave entrance, was handed over to the Belize Department of Archeology, Belmopan. May 3, 1972.

* * * * *

During the 1972 National Day Celebrations I traveled to Orange Walk to assist with a track and field meet. On Friday morning, September 8, I piled borrowed equipment into a requisitioned ministry truck and by that afternoon was with organizers of the meet in Orange Walk, laying out the field. Competition was scheduled for the next day. That evening I stayed with PCV Neil Policelli and his wife Tony, who were now living and working in

Yo Creek, located about six miles west of Orange Walk.

The next day there was a big downpour in the morning and the track meet was cancelled. After securing equipment from the field, Neil took me back to Yo Creek where I stay the rest of the weekend.

At that time a man named Don Warren was managing a 25,000-acre mango farm near Yo Creek. An American company called Carver Tropical Products financed the project.[3] Don was a friend of Neil and Tony's, and invited us to his home for lunch on Sunday. He lived sixteen miles west of Yo Creek in a thatched house he had built. The dwelling had a cement floor and screened windows. Don said there was a rat problem and showed me various gunshot holes he had made through the roof and walls when eliminating the pests.

After lunch we traveled farther west to a Mennonite community called Blue Creek, which is on the border with Mexico. Before getting there, we stopped and went swimming at a nice swimming hole where two rivers converge. At Blue Creek, a river separates the two countries. On the Mexican side is a community called La Unión.

104. *Don Warren, PCVs Tony and Neil Policelli, and the author swimming at Dos Bocas on the road to Blue Creek. September 10, 1972.*

105. *Near La Unión. A Mexican military outpost across the river from the Mennonite village. September 10, 1972.*

Bamboo Playground

While serving in Sierra Leone (1969-1971), I came across a UNESCO[4] booklet from East Africa that explained how to construct playground equipment using bamboo and old tires. The pamphlet was written as part of an inquiry-based booklet series used to teach science in third world elementary schools. Using the information as a guide, I worked with interested primary schools in Bo Town to construct climbing towers and swings from native bamboo (Picture 5, Page 10).

In 1972 PCV Rick Sharp arrived in British Honduras to teach physical education at Belize Teachers' College. I told Rick about the playground booklet and together we showed his college students how to use bamboo for this purpose.

The closest bamboo forest to Belize City was in an area known as Gracie Rock, a small community about twenty miles west of town. One weekend we borrowed the Peace Corps truck and went there to collect what bamboo was needed. The following pictures were taken during that project.

Ted W. Cox

106. Gracie Rock. PVC Rick Sharp cutting bamboo in front of the Peace Corps truck. October 21, 1972.

107. Gracie Rock. Instructor PCV Rick Sharp collecting bamboo for Belize Teachers' College project. October 21, 1972.

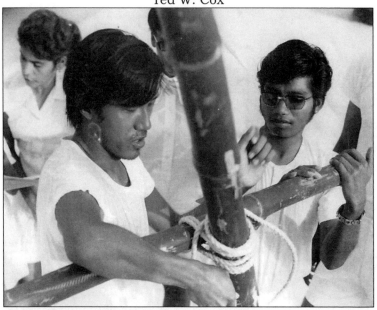

108. Belize City. College students constructing a climbing tower. November 9, 1972.

Ted W. Cox

109. Belize City. The author supervising construction. November 9, 1972.

110. Belize City. Belize Teachers' College students during construction of the tower. November 9, 1972.

111. Belize City. Belize Teachers' College. Instructor PCV Rick Sharp officiates volleyball game with his students. November 9, 1972.

15
Notes

[1] Obituary for Albert L. Bevis, 1911-2008. Patterson Cemetery District, California Genealogy and History Archives. August 11, 2008.

[2] Mennonite founder Menno Simmons was originally a Catholic priest from the Netherlands who joined and then split from the Anabaptist movement in 1536. His followers were called Mennonites.

During 1958, Mennonites emigrated from Canada and Mexico to British Honduras to establish a new home. Part of the reason they adopted Belize was because there was so much potential good land for farming. They turned sections of rural Belize into highly productive farmland and dairies. Hard working and innovative, the Mennonites had established themselves firmly, both economically and in the good will of all Belizean people, by 1972.

[3] According to Governor Posnett, mangoes were exported to the U.S. from Belize and used as a thickener for Campbell's soups.

[4] UNESCO (United Nations Educational, Scientific and Cultural Organization) was created in 1945. The organization strives to provide quality education to all children, to protect world heritage sites and to support cultural diversity around the world.

16
Girlfriends
Baron Bliss

Baron Henry Bliss (1869-1926) was a wealthy Englishman who inherited his title from Portugal. He traveled to British Honduras on his own luxury yacht in 1926 and found the fishing to his liking. Bliss met many Belizeans during his maritime visit, experiencing good relationships as well as agreeable weather. Unfortunately, due to failing health, he died only four months after arriving. Before passing away, he bequeathed a two-million-dollar trust gift to the colony.

Today the Baron Bliss Trust Fund is available for numerous projects that continually benefit Belizeans. His endowment made possible the building of the locally famous Bliss Institute Library and Museum in 1953.[1]

112. Belize City. Bliss Institute houses a theatre for the performing arts, a museum, a library and the University of the West Indies. 1975.

In September 1971, as a newly arrived PCV, I enrolled in an adult education Spanish class at the Bliss Institute where I first saw Leni Jo Usher. A striking woman, she was an instructor teaching remedial math and English at the institute. Later that month, while visiting St. John's College where she taught English, I introduced myself. And so a relationship began. Both of us were quite busy, but she enthusiastically found time to introduce me to her friends and family in Belize City. We enjoyed each other's company and she loved sports. As a youth, her father was a star basketball athlete in Belize City, and she herself was quite active in sports during her high school years.

When it came to pride in family and country, she was zealous and loyal to the bone but not assertive about her thoughts unless asked or confronted.

Ted W. Cox

113. Belize City. The author and Leni Jo Usher. November 1971.

Leni Jo took time from her schedule to help me coordinate a number of track and field events during 1972. However, by June, we began drifting apart. The biggest problem from my perspective was that we were both extremely stubborn and often argued. At first my heart was broken. One

199

day at the Social Development Office, transportation driver Robert Mitchell saw me sulking (Picture 114). He smiled and said, "Ted, Macobie de pan you." I was puzzled by this comment and he repeated, "Macobie de pan you, mon." His remark got a big laugh from the staff. Mitchell was talking Creole, telling me that I had a broken heart. According to Belizean friend Dave Anderson, there are three stages of love sickness:
1. *macobie* – broken heart
2. *jeng jeng* – when you get mad
3. *kabanka* – when you hurt so much you want to kill yourself

Lucky for me I stopped at macobie.

Even with our setbacks, we remained friends and Leni Jo continued to assist me with the BHAAA. After over thirty-five years of lost contact, Leni Jo was one of the most recent supporters to edit and encourage completion of this manuscript.

In early December 1972, at the suggestion of Bill Lightburn, I bought conch shellfish at the central market. The seafood, a delicacy, was in season. Bill offered to grind up the conch at his house on Euphrates Avenue, and gave me a recipe for making fritters. Later that same day while at my apartment, I made some batter and mixed in the ground conch, creating cakes that were then stored in my freezer.

Ted W. Cox

114. Belize City. Robert Mitchell, Ministry of Social Development driver. March 23, 1973.

On Saturday, December 16, the fritters were pulled out of the freezer to thaw while I went off to play a rugby match at the Airport Camp. Following the game I went home and fried up the fritters and ate my fill. Apparently, my refrigeration, food handling and frying skills needed some refining.

That evening, I went to a Cable and Wireless Company Christmas party with Patsy Monroe, an attractive young woman I had asked to come with me. I returned home early as my stomach was feeling a bit troubled, so I went to bed and after a short time, food poisoning hit. This was a bad case of food poisoning. I was by myself, in terrible pain with uncontrollable bowels. To get to the toilet was a struggle. I began throwing up in pain for what seemed an eternity. My stomach felt like it was being rubbed with a dry hand. No telephone and too weak to holler for help. Why did I not die? It was just not my time. The following day, Sunday, was also a bad day, and still no one knew of my condition. By Monday morning I was in somewhat of a recovery mode and gradually came back to life.

There are some advantages to being young and healthy, but none for being young and stupid.

115. *Belize City. Left to right: Patsy Monroe, Betty Fairweather, Gilda Deeks and Sistie Fairweather. The picture was taken in front of the Fairweather home on Freetown Road, also the location of Sistie's Dance Studio. 1973.*

Patsy Monroe, with whom I unfairly associate the above-mentioned culinary disaster, was a member of Sistie's Dance Studio in Belize City.

Barbara (Fairweather) Harris, was Sistie's sister and the Peace Corps secretary. She became one of my best Belizean friends. Barbara lived next door to her parents with her husband, Neil, and their two children, Francis and Lydia. Sistie ran the dance studio next door on the lower floor of their parents' house.

Sistie had students of various ages who performed at the Bliss Center for Performing Arts and at international venues. The troupe continued until 1977, when Sistie left Belize to live in the United States.[2]

116. *Belize City. Sistie's Dance Studio performing at the Bliss Institute. Lydia Harris, arms folded, bottom row third from right, and Terry Fairweather, top row third from right, facing the camera with bright eyes. May 6, 1973.*

117. Bliss Institute. Sistie's Dance Studio. Shaun Stewart waiting to dance to "Bud Benk Wedding."[3] May 6, 1973.

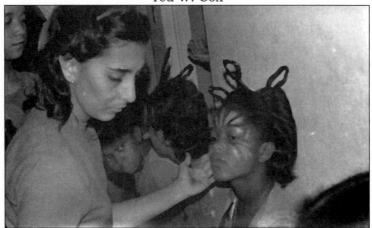

118. Bliss Institute. Solie Arguellas of Studio Dansol applying makeup. May 6, 1973.

Baron Bliss stipulated in his 1926 will that a portion of the trust be spent each year for a river regatta. Every March a three-day weekend celebrates this event in his honor.

Journal
March 9,1972 – Thursday
Belize City

Baron Bliss Day Celebrations
Today is an annual holiday in British Honduras celebrating the life of the country's greatest benefactor, Baron Bliss. During the holiday, popular boat races are held on Haulover Creek in Belize City. In the afternoon I went to the celebrations and took some pictures.

119. Belize City. Baron Bliss River Regatta on Haulover Creek. March 9, 1972.

120. Belize City. Competitors finish the race. March 9, 1972.

121. Belize City. Baron Bliss River Regatta on Haulover Creek. At the finish line. March 9, 1972.

Plays were also held at the Bliss Insitute. In June 1973, I went to see *Bamboo Clump*, directed and acted in by my friend Frank Cervantes.

122. Belize City. Bliss Institute. Bamboo Clump *director/actor Frank Cervantes with two friends. June 17, 1973.*

123. Belize City. Bliss Institute. Bamboo Clump *director/actor Frank Cervantes during a scene in the play. June 17, 1973.*

16
Notes

[1] Other accomplishments completed in the past century with Bliss trust funds include:

The Bliss School of Nursing
Belize City water supply system
In-transit lounge at the Belize International
  Airport
Land purchase to build Belmopan
Construction of the Burdon Canal in 1929.
   This canal opened a safe route for farmers between Belize City and the South Belize District.

[2] In 1996, Sistie (Fairweather) Harmes returned to Belize where she continues sharing her passion for modern dance through Vista Dance Studio in Ladyville.

[3] Check out Lord Rhaburn singing this song on YouTube. It's easy to imagine Shaun dancing to this catchy tune.

17
The Cayo District

Ted W. Cox

124. Entering San Ignacio over the Hawkesworth Bridge. PCV Chris Dixon is standing on the left. January 1973.

On Saturday, January 15, 1972, I met with primary school representatives in San Ignacio to discuss the organization of an inter-primary school field day planned for March. This was apparently the first time an inter-school competition had been organized, so I was quite excited to be involved. Among those present were Hernan Ochaeta (St. Andrew's Primary), Mrs. Lileth Perdomo, Jose Zuniga and Neville Young.

One order of business was the need to upgrade the town field. Mayor E. Luna asked me for the measurements needed to lay out a 400-meter track. During this visit to town, I also arranged a meeting between principals, teachers and interested citizens regarding the Western Divisional Secondary School Track and Field Meet between Belmopan Comprehensive and Western High School.

On January 17, I traveled to San Ignacio with Belmopan High School Principal Sister Sarita, along with Steve Panky and Ed Henderson. We met with Western High School Principal Salizar, Dave Cruz and Adrian Levy. The meeting seemed promising, but unfortunately Western High School did not take part in the 1972 event.

Journal
March 13, 1972 – Monday
San Ignacio

Left Belize City at 5:30 a.m. for San Ignacio with Mr. Mitchell in Ministry of Local Government Land Rover #5300. Met with San Ignacio Mayor Luna and got permission to work on city field developing a running track with six of his men after lunch. We worked until 6 p.m.

Mr. L. Waight, the district officer, said that he would order a grader on Saturday to level new soil on the field if I would return from Belize City to advise. I said that I would.

I attended a meeting at the courthouse at 6:30 p.m. regarding the organization of the upcoming inter-primary school field day.

Met with Mr. Jose Zuniga and Josephine Recinos. That night I slept at the Government Rest House.

Next morning I took a bus to Belmopan for 50 cents, and from there caught a ride to Belize City with my Belizean boss, Mr. Carl Coleman.

Ted W. Cox

125. San Ignacio. Preparing the city field for the March 24 Inter-Primary School Field Day. The Hawkesworth Bridge is visible in the background. March 13, 1972.

126. *San Ignacio. Preparing the city field for the March 24 Inter-Primary School Field Day. March 13, 1972.*

127. *San Ignacio. Before the Belize Telecommunications Authority was established in 1972, a call from San Ignacio to Belize City had to be made through this telephone exchange.1971.*

Journal
March 18, 1972 – Saturday
San Ignacio

Left Belize City at 7:30 a.m. in Ministry of Local Government Land Rover to San Ignacio. Mr. Mitchell was driving. Before leaving we picked up Leni Jo and James Usher.

After reaching San Ignacio we went to the city field and saw that about $200 of infill had been dropped on the lower section. The district officer, Mr. L. Waight, was at the mayor's office and said a bulldozer would arrive by 1 p.m. for the leveling.

Saw Father Martin. He told me that his school would not take part in the upcoming inter-secondary school track meet.

We had lunch at Eva's Restaurant. A drunken man sweet-talked Leni Jo in Spanish. After lunch, our driver took Leni Jo to visit the Mayan ruins at Xunantunich near Benque Viejo. James and I waited for the bulldozer, which arrived by 2 p.m. The bulldozer started leveling the track, but then unexpectedly left to work on Hector Silva's horse track.

While waiting for the bulldozer to return, James and I went swimming in the Macal River that runs through the town. By 5 p.m. Leni and Mitch returned from the ruins and came down to the riverside to see us.

The grader finally arrived so I went to the field to take some pictures, and then went over to the D.O.'s house. I told him that I would send the grader pictures so he could post them in his office for publicity. We left for Belize City, and on the way Mitchell took a detour through Belmopan since Leni Jo had not visited the new capital before. We reached Belize City by 10 p.m.

*128. San Ignacio. District Officer L. Waight's house.
March 18, 1972.*

Journal
March 23, 1972 – Thursday
San Ignacio

Traveled from Belize City to San Ignacio at
10:00 a.m. on public bus for $1.25. Arrived at 2:00
p.m. and went to the mayor's office. The district
officer was there. The mayor thanked me for the
nice comment that I made about him on Sunday's
radio sports report.

The mayor said that from the time I
completed my coaches clinic in January, they had
not received any support from the public works, so
the primary school competition would be held in
the football stadium.

129. *San Ignacio Inter-Primary School Field Day.*
Politician Hector Silva is on the left. March 24, 1972.

Journal
March 24, 1972 – Friday
San Ignacio

I got up at 6:00 a.m. and went to the football field, where we finished marking the track. The events started about 9:30 a.m. after an opening talk by PUP politician Hector Silva. The meet went very smooth, lasting until 12:00. Then a break and resumed again at 12:45 until 3:00 p.m. Thirty events were conducted.

This was San Ignacio's first inter-school field day and I was pleased my advice was used and that things went smoothly.

I caught a ride to Belize City with a convoy of Guatemalan trucks carrying Orange Crush.

18
Yo Creek
Inter-Primary School
Field Day

On Saturday, May 20, 1972, I traveled north to Yo Creek in Orange Walk District. There I met with principals and teachers of local elementary schools, a number of whom had taken my track and field course described in Chapter Eight. An inter-school field day was scheduled to take place on the following Tuesday starting at 9 a.m. I was invited to stay with PCVs Neil and Tony Policelli at their home in Yo Creek. That Sunday, Neil and I spent most of the day helping to lay out the running track, assisted by teachers who had taken the clinic in January.

Journal
May 20, 1972
Yo Creek

PCV Bill Cain and I caught a ride to Yo Creek with Kelly Compton, the Assistant Peace Corps Director. Kelly was checking on how Volunteers in the field were doing. I was coming to help run an inter-primary school field day on the 23rd.

On Tuesday, ten primary schools took part in the event, with the minister of education announcing the opening ceremony. All of the contestants were elementary school children.

Ted W. Cox

130. Yo Creek. PCV Tony Policelli, PCV Bill Cain, and Assistant Peace Corps Director Kelly Compton. May 20, 1972.

Ted W. Cox

131. Yo Creek. Inter-Primary School Field Day. Ten schools participated. May 23, 1972.

Ted W. Cox

132. Yo Creek. PCV Neil Policelli helped as starter. May 23, 1972.

133. Yo Creek. Relay race. May 23, 1972.

134. Yo Creek. Long jump. May 23, 1972.

135. Yo Creek. Long jump. May 23, 1972.

136. Yo Creek. Recording scores. May 23, 1972.

137.Yo Creek. James Usher from Belize City presents awards. May 23, 1972.

138. Yo Creek. Boys gather for a picture. May 23, 1972.

139.Yo Creek. Girls show off their latest fashions. May 23, 1972.

19
Triangular Track and Field Meet, 1972

Revival of the Triangular Track and Field Meet in 1972 involved the Amateur Athletic Association, the Police Special Forces and the resident British garrison. Historically, the competition drew large crowds at the MCC Grounds. The meet had already been postponed twice due to weather and other reasons. This time, a second venue option if the MCC Grounds had not been available on June 11 was the Airport Camp. Tickets for the public were priced at 15 and 35 cents.

Ted W. Cox

140. *The author, Sergeant Winston Carcano, British Honduras Police, and Gilmore Hinkson[1], treasurer BHAAA, discuss upcoming Triangular Track and Field Meet. April 1972.*

Letter Home
June 9, 1972
Belize City

Dear Mother,
    The rains are starting to come now. I spent the last three days at the MCC sport grounds preparing the athletic field. This coming Sunday the biggest track meet of the year: British Army vs Belize Police vs Amateur Athletic Association, weather permitting.
    The Grenadier Guards have been very co-operative the last six months and have helped me get some track and field equipment.

Ted W. Cox

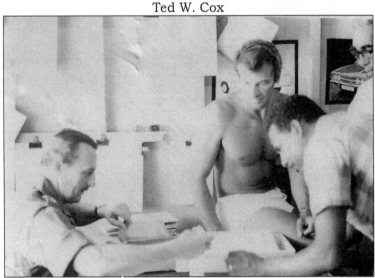

141. Lt. Bob Woodfield and Sgt. Dick Slater of the Grenadier Guards talk with BHAA President Norrin O. Meighan and Gilmore Hinkson about the upcoming Triangular Track and Field Meet scheduled on June 11, 1972.

Journal
June 8, 1972 – Thursday
Belize City

Got up at 5 a.m. Sergeant Allen Hughes came from the Airport Camp and we worked preparing the MCC Grounds for army elimination competition until 8 a.m. The eliminations lasted all day. Afterwards the Amateur Athletic Association athletes conducted qualifying events.

Journal
June 11, 1972
Belize City

The Triangular Track and Field Meet was held today. Everything went smooth. There were a large number of spectators. The meet, originally scheduled for March 11, had been postponed for three months.

Ted W. Cox

142. Belize City. British Honduras Volunteer Guard Band was originally formed in 1947 as a drum and bugle corps. In 1952 it added a brass section. Since 1981 it has been known as the Belize Defense Force Band. Gilmore Hinkson and Winston Carcano stand in foreground at MCC Grounds. 1972.

143. Belize City. MCC Grounds. Presenting the team flags. June 11, 1972.

*144. Triangular Track Meet distance race.
Grenadier Guards are all wearing similar jerseys
with dark logos on the front. June 11, 1972.*

145. *Soldier uses radio transmitter to relay results to the officials' box. June 11, 1972.*

146. *Another view of officials gathered at the finish line. June 11, 1972.*

232

147. *Steve Perera (center), representing BHAAA, shakes hands with a Grenadier during the awards ceremony. June 11, 1972.*

148. *The governor's wife, Mrs. Shirley Posnett, hands an award to James Usher for the medley race. From left are Michael Hyde, Phylip Andrewin and E. Morris. June 11, 1972.*

149. BHAAA javelin thrower. June 11, 1972.

150. Grenadier clearing the bar and landing on donated garrison mattresses. June 11, 1972.

151. The Fosbury Flop style of high jump was first introduced internationally by Dick Fosbury during the 1968 Mexico Olympic Games. June 11, 1972.

152. Fred Henry competes in the shot put event for the BHAAA. June 11, 1972.

153. Grenadier tug of war team gives its best. June 11, 1972.

The BHAAA gave a strong performance, but the Grenadiers won the meet by a narrow margin in the closing minutes.

Later that year, following their deployment in British Honduras, the Grenadiers won the London District Track Meet and the Southern Command Championship in Great Britain.[2]

19
Notes

1 Written on the brown envelope (lower front of the book cover), is the signature of Gilmore Hinkson, Belize Postal Inspector.

2 Oliver Lindsay, *Once a Grenadier – The Grenadier Guards 1945-1995* (London: Leo Cooper, 1996), 199.

20
Heading for the States

On June 30, 1972, I took an official Peace Corps midterm vacation and left the country to visit family in Ontario, California. Land travel by bus from Belize City to Tijuana, including food, was about $60 US at that time. From Belize City, my first stop was Corozal, Belize. Across the border in Chetumal, arrangements were made for the Mexican travel visa. Officials took a serious look at my passport, perhaps checking to see if I was on a wanted list. This didn't take long, but before issuing the visa they said I had to have a vaccination. Not happy about this requirement, I found my options were to cut the trip short or move on. I decided to move on and took the injection.

At the bus station in Chetumal, I purchased an A.D.O. (Autotransportes de Oriente) bus ticket to Mexico City for the following day, then passed the night at a hotel.

After boarding the bus in the morning, I found myself sitting next to a Belize Creole lady who was going to attempt to enter the United States illegally. The term used by Belizeans sneaking into the U.S via Mexico was "going through the back". She did not have a plan as to how to cross the border.

239

After an eighteen-hour ride we arrived in Mexico City and immediately left on a different bus line, called Transporte del Norte. The ticket to Tijuana cost 271 pesos ($23 US).

When we reached Tijuana, it was 4:30 a.m. July 4. I knew my Belizean acquaintance was in for a tough time but hesitated to involve my family in trying to drive her across the border. So I showed her where the crossing was and wished success. About six months later, while I was working in Belmopan, I saw the same lady. She was employed as a nurse's aide. She said that after we parted in Tijuana, she attempted to cross the border in the afternoon and was immediately stopped by a U.S. Immigration officer, who sent her back to Belize.

To her misfortune, the bus going back through Mexico was robbed by bandits. Apparently, one of the bandits was riding as a passenger and asked to get off at a certain isolated location. At that point armed bandits entered the bus. She lost all the possessions she was carrying with her.

After crossing into the U.S. I called my sister Janis and her husband, Ed. They had driven the family down to Mission Bay near San Diego to meet me when the bus arrived. They stayed in a hotel there with my mother and two nieces, Carole and Sandra.

154. San Diego, California. My mother, Florence, and sister Janis. July 4, 1972.

155. San Diego. Janis and her daughter Sandra talk to a celebrity filming a Dodge TV commercial. July 5, 1972.

Prior to leaving for the states, I made arrangements to work a few days for Smithford Products, a previous employer in Ontario. The business, which opened in late 1965, was located just south of the old Ontario International Airport. They produced mostly aluminum castings for the defense aerospace industry. Nolan Ford, co-owner, originally hired me in 1966, when I was nineteen years old. He soon took a liking to me and suggested that I take some metallurgy courses to learn more about the business, but I was not interested in foundry work as a career.

156. Ontario, California. The old sign from 1966 and the company buildings were still standing but deserted in this October 2013 photo.

The day I showed up for work in 1972, Nolan told me in private that the company had just recently become exceedingly profitable. These were the Vietnam years and the business had obtained prized government defense contracts.

One of the castings manufactured was used with napalm bombs that were shackled under the wings of aircraft supporting ground troops. I had worked on hundreds of these during the summer of 1966. At the start of production there were quality control issues, and I was sent to re-work casting delivered at the bomb plant in

157. Ontario, California. Smithford Products co-worker cleaning aluminum casting using compressed air. His father was born into slavery in 1860! This fact brought living history into acute perspective for me. July 1972.

the City of Industry. As I write these memoirs in 2013, I can't help but wonder if I might have worked in a factory that eventually supplied materials sent to the Guatemalan Air Force!

Sometime after returning to British Honduras, I received word that Nolan Ford had died from a heart attack.

After over forty years, the company he had started with Warren Smith in 1965 officially closed in 2009.

On July 31, Janis and Ed drove me back to the Mexican border where I walked across to Tijuana and bought a bus ticket for Mexico City, leaving that same evening at 6:00 p.m.

Seeing my family, those that I love, was a real treat. Being in Southern California was another matter. My visit confirmed that all the smog and population was something to be avoided. For me, Southern California is a great place to visit, but not to live.

Journal
August 2, 1972
Mexico City

When I arrived in Mexico City via Transporte del Norte, I immediately went to the A.D.O. bus ticket counter to purchase a bus ticket south. The ticket seller said that there were no seats available to Chetumal until Saturday, so I bought the ticket. I was concerned because my cash was limited.

A taxi driver took me to the San Carlo where I booked a room for two nights at $12 a night. The San Carlo is located in the center of the city across from Revolutionary Monument. After cleaning up, I got something to eat at a nearby restaurant, and there I met three Mexican businessmen. One of them spoke English and could see that I was a foreigner. He invited me to join them. They were curious about the United States Peace Corps and had many questions. The three took me to accompany them to Garibaldi Plaza where we drank till 3 a.m. and listened to mariachi music.

Journal
August 4, 1972
Mexico City

I got up at 9:00 a.m. and walked around the city center and saw a British volunteer from Corozal who had taken my track and field course. I went back to the San Carlo and slept until 3 p.m. and then checked out. I took my bags to store at the bus station.

At this point I was without money for a room to sleep in for the night. Mexico City is located at a high elevation and I was not prepared for a chilly night. I went to two movies, and spent the rest of the night between the A.D.O. station and an all night restaurant. Morning finally came, and when it was time to board the bus, I was told at the ticket counter that all the seats were already taken, and I would have to wait a few more days. At this point I started to panic and made my way to the bus that was going to the Yucatan. The driver said that there was room and I immediately got on the bus.

I arrived in Chetumal on the border of British Honduras at 10:30 a.m. The day was Sunday and I was lucky to meet up with a chartered Belizean taxi that was returning to Corozal. In Corozal I located a truck driver who was heading for Belize City at 2:00 p.m. and arrived home by 5:30 p.m.

158. Corozal waterfront. The building on the far right was the public market. 1973.

21
The Fairweathers
Arrival of the
Devon and Dorset Regiment

A few days after returning to Belize, I paid a visit to the Fairweather residence on Freetown Road. This is the house where Sistie's Dance Studio was located. Colonel D.N.A. Fairweather, Barbara's father, was a respected elder who joined the British Honduras Volunteer Guard in 1939 and was Commandant from 1947 to 1963. During our conversation he showed me the draft of a booklet he was writing about the guard.[1]

In 1956 he led a march with eighteen guardsmen down the coast towards Punta Gorda. They came upon a Mayan Indian village not indicated on his map. When questioned, the village leader said that they had fled Guatemala to settle there because the Guatemalan Army was taking away their men each year and forcing them into military service.

In another story, he told me of a Guatemalan colonel who asked to meet with him in Benque Viejo del Carmen in 1962. Benque Viejo is near the Guatemalan border on the road to Tikal. The Guatemalan colonel asked Fairweather to supply him with arms and ammunition to support a revolution. Colonel Fairweather refused to cooperate and reported the incident to the governor.

DNA Fairweather Collection

159. Lt. Colonel D.N.A. Fairweather (1899-1985). British Honduras Volunteer Guard, 1939-63.

160. Belize City. Peace Corps Office Administrator Barbara (Fairweather) Harris with her children Francis and Lydia. Their home on Freetown Road was located next to the home of her father, Lt. Colonel D.N.A. Fairweather. November 1972.

161. Airport Camp. Belize City vs Grenadier Guards rugby match. Belize City 8 – Army 12. The author is in the front row. March 28, 1972.

Journal
August 19, 1972
Belize City

Went to Airport Camp to play a rugby game against the new resident infantry, the 1st Battalion Devon and Dorset Regiment. We lost 40 to 4. Dinner and beer was hosted by the army afterwards and melted away the sting of defeat.

The popular drink on the field after the game was Tennyson beer mixed with 7-Up and referred to as shandy.

The Grenadier Guards left the country, following a twelve-month extended deployment. They were replaced by the 1st Battalion Devon and Dorset Regiment, beginning August 1972. The new regiment began its job with the usual military reconnaissance, rehearsing emergency deployment plans, and beginning jungle training. All of this preparation helped the officers assess the threat level from Guatemala.

As part of the British Army's aid to the Belizean community, this batch of soldiers took a "can do" attitude and identified dozens of areas of need in the country. They were like Peace Corps Volunteers with no less than twenty-five projects completed during their brief six-month stay. The accomplishments of the battalion led to recognition from Governor Posnett and to the Wilkinson Sword of Peace award for 1972.[2]

Each company had its own project in places like Punta Gorda, Paraiso, San Pedro, San Miguel, Orange Walk, Corozal, and San Ignacio. Medical teams visited remote villages that were beyond the reach of local services. They taught hygiene, prevented an outbreak of measles, painted a school, conducted a population census for a remote village, and taught physical education in schools. Their most ambitious project was rebuilding a bridge in the Kekchi Mayan village of San Miguel. This community is located in the south, where a river called the Rio Grande splits the village from its agricultural land on the opposite bank. In 1972, a rickety old bridge spanned the river. To rebuild was beyond village capabilities, so an officer and eighteen men, after receiving guidance from the Royal Engineers, built a new bridge in eighteen days.[3]

When soldiers were not on reconnaissance, jungle exercises, field firing, or training in navigation, Belize could be an adventure playground. What a posting! A soldier could spend his off time drinking rum and Coke and diving in the blue waters of the Caribbean. In addition to local excursions, soldiers from various regiments took holiday visits to Merida, Cancun, Chetumal, and even played in rugby tournaments in Mexico City.

Rick Sharp, a fellow Peace Corps Volunteer in 1972, said of the soldiers he knew:

Rick: They were really fun to be with. They would be drinking, playing rugby and go out on tactics. They were probably happy to get out of England where it would be cold and overcast and chilly. Plus they probably didn't want to work in the coal mines. Many didn't have a variety of job opportunities back home.

Those guys had more fun in Belize. One time when I was leaving Airport Camp after a rugby game, I looked over to one of those little quonset huts where the soldiers lived. There was this big tiger skin stretched out. It looked like somebody had shot and killed a tiger, maybe out on maneuvers or tactics, and skinned it. This big skin, like a bear skin rug, stretched out in front of the little barracks. It was the darnedest thing.

Ted W. Cox

162. Airport Camp. Rick Sharp jumps high in line out during a rugby contest between Belize City and the Devon and Dorset Regiment. We lost again. December 9, 1972.

21
Notes

[1] D.N.A. Fairweather, "A Short History of the Volunteer Forces of British Honduras (Now Belize)," 1978. Self published.

[2] The Wilkinson Sword of Peace Award was established in 1966 by British sword maker Wilkinson Sword and given to units of the British Armed Forces for activities that improved relations with the communites where they were deployed.

[3] www. keepmilitarymuseum.org

22
Physical Performance Testing

In December 1971, I recommended to the ministry that a national physical performance survey of secondary schools be conducted. The idea was suggested to me while visiting the Physical Education Graduate School at Eastern Illinois University three months earlier.[1]

The ministry was told that published results could be used as a tool for teachers and clubs to motivate the youth and discover individuals with exceptional physical skills. In the United States, the battery of tests was first conducted in 1958 and remained popular for twenty-two years, with only minor changes. In 1980 a health-related fitness test replaced the performance fitness test.

The tests included seven challenges that evaluated basic components of fitness: strength, speed, agility, endurance, power and throwing skill. They were uncomplicated for an instructor to administer with minimum equipment. A manual would compare percentage tables so students could immediately see how they performed when compared to other students in the country. The objective of the survey as presented to the ministry was twofold. First, to administer a battery of physical performance tests to Belizean students and establish national norms. Second, to publish the results in a booklet to be made available to Belizean teachers and interested civic groups.

The following excerpt is taken from the report submitted to the ministry:

Minister of Local Government - Community and Social Development
December 21, 1971.

C. Physical Fitness Testing

Physical fitness testing is used in the United States to measure the physical standard of the nation's young, to locate weaknesses and to create an awareness of program effectiveness. Skills tested have a relationship to performance in track and field. These tests can be administered in schools or other programs to stimulate physical activity for sports in general.

I would like to suggest that a national physical performance test be conducted throughout the country to establish Belizean standards that can be used to motivate the youth. Testing could be conducted from September through December 1972.

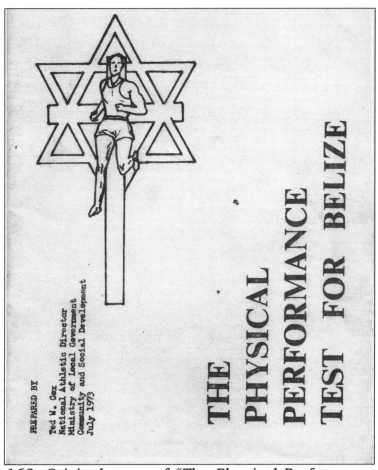

163. Original cover of "The Physical Performance Test for Belize." July 1973.

Both the Ministry of Local Government and Ministry of Education gave approval for the project in June 1972. At that time Belize had a total of twenty secondary schools, three of which were exclusively female. Total enrollment of all schools, boys and girls in forms one through four (ninth to twelfth grade) in 1971 was estimated to be 3,506.[2]

In order to organize a testing schedule, an explanation of the program was first mailed to all secondary schools. The following letter was typical of the responses received from principals regarding the project:

The Methodist Church Honduras District
Fletcher College

16th November 1972
P.O. Box 65
Corozal Town

Mr. Ted W. Cox
Track and Field Director
Social Development Department
P.O. Box 41
Belize City

Dear Ted,

In answer to your letter of November 10, we would be glad to have you come to Fletcher College to conduct the tests on Physical fitness. There are a total of 21 boys in Form I and 21 boys in Form II.

There will be at least one staff member available to assist you during these tests, so that in future years we will be able to conduct the tests without assistance.

Looking forward to your visit.

Sincerely,
Antonio J. Correa,
Principal

---

* * * * *

During January 1973, I traveled to Orange Walk to administer the Physical Performance Test at Muffles College. While there, I could not resist climbing the new telephone tower with the plan to take some pictures from the top. The climb was accomplished after I finished one of the fitness tests; some students came to the top with me.

Ted W. Cox

164.Orange Walk. Solomon Constanza (salesman for British Fidelity Insurance) climbing inside the new telecommunications tower. January 31,1973.

165. Orange Walk as seen from the new telecommunications tower. The New River is located in the upper center of the picture. January 31, 1973.

Journal
March 22, 1973
Orange Walk

Took early bus to Orange Walk. Ticket cost $1.25. In Orange Walk the bus driver dropped me by the convent. Sister Leona said that I could stay in the convent for the night, sleeping in her office. I had supper with the nuns. While eating they said that about 100 Mennonites were about to leave British Honduras for Bolivia. They wanted to start a new life there. Mostly young settlers.

Sister Leona said she had climbed to the top of the 400-ft. telephone tower about two weeks ago. Sister James only got about half way. Then a day or so later the sister in charge of their provincial chapter was visiting from the United States. She inquired about the new telephone tower. They told her about it and said they had climbed up. About ten minutes later it just so happened an official from the telecommunications company came to the convent and said in front of everyone, "Sister, would you do me a favor – please ask your students not to climb the tower."

The next day she addressed the student body telling the students to refrain from climbing, Sister Leona said, "We have been loose about climbing the tower."

The Sister was blushing when telling us this story, and we all had a good laugh.

Over 1,000 students from fifteen schools eventually took part in the survey that was conducted between October 1972 and March 1973. Belize City, being the main center of population with the largest number of secondary schools, was chosen as the starting point. The survey began in the fall of 1972. Testing in the out district began January 1973.

The survey followed standards used in the 1958 "United States Youth Fitness Test." The test battery consisted of the following:

1. Pull-up for boys (for judging arm and shoulder girdle strength).

2. Straight leg sit-up (for judging strength and endurance of abdominal and hip flexor muscles).

3. Shuttle run (for judging speed and change of direction).

4. Standing broad jump (for judging explosive muscle power of leg extensors).

5. 50-yard dash (for judging speed).

6. Softball throw (for judging skill and coordination).

7. 600-yard run-walk (for judging cardiovascular efficiency).

Due to time constraints and the larger number of male students available, testing was limited basically to first and second form boys (ninth and tenth grade).

The original sit-up test had been modified in 1965 in the United States using a bent leg. In Belize, I used the 1958 U.S. format to ensure valid comparisons between the two countries.

Ted W. Cox

166. Belize City. Belize Technical College. Pull-up. Tested by Ronald Lewis and Morrell Gillette. October 12, 1972.

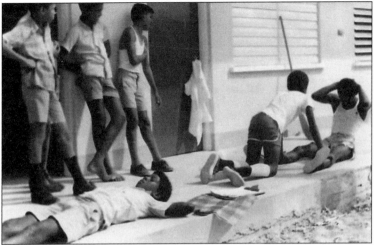

167. Belize City. Junior Secondary #2. Form 1-5. Sit-up. November 3, 1972.

168. Stann Creek. Austin High. Shuttle run. February 27, 1973.

169. Belize City. St. John's College. Standing broad jump. Tested by Eric Neal. October 6, 1972.

170. Orange Walk. Muffles College. 50-yard dash. January 30, 1973.

Ted W.Cox

171. San Ignacio. Western High School. Softball throw. January 10, 1973.

Ted W. Cox

172. Belmopan. Belmopan Comprehensive. 600-yard run-walk. January 22, 1973.

Belize City schools that took part in the testing were:

1. St. John's College
   120 first form boys, 120 second form boys
2. Belize Technical College
   50 second form boys
3. Belize Junior Secondary #1
   40 first form boys, 40 second form boys
4. Belize Junior Secondary #2
   62 first form boys
5. Nazarene
   15 first form boys, 7 second form boys
6. Michael's College
   48 first form boys
   45 second form boys

Out district schools that took part in the testing included:

7. Western High School, San Ignacio
   58 first form boys
   25 second form boys
8. Belmopan Comprehensive, Belmopan
   33 first form boys
   20 second form boys
9. Muffles College, Orange Walk
   45 first form boys
   36 second form boys
10. Xavier College, Corozal
    38 first form boys
    18 second form boys

11. Fletcher College, Corozal
    17 first form boys
    21 second form boys
    15 third form boys
12. Austin High School, Stann Creek
    48 first form boys
    20 second form boys
13. Stann Creek High School, Stann
    Creek
    29 first form boys
    29 second form boys
14. St. Peter Claver, Punta Gorda
    15 first form boys
    17 second form boys
15. St. Peter's College, San Pedro
    9 first form boys

Following months of collecting data, PCV Neal Hammond helped convert the findings into meaningful charts at the Peace Corps Office in Belize City during May 1973:

Neal: Well, I remember that we used one of the first calculators on the market. It was actually a statistical calculator. We were able to do what seemed to us at the time miraculous. At the touch of a button get standard deviations and do all of the calculations.

The Peace Corps bought this calculator for me. I had requested it. At the time the Peace Corps had a limited amount of funds to help the volunteers. There was about $1000 available.

Yeah, we could put your numbers in and I think we did that at the Peace Corps Office. There were no computers then, but we did have some calculation ability. It was a Texas Instrument calculator. One of the first with digital output.

The data was compared with similar results from the United States. American youth tended to perform better in the sit-up, 50-yard dash and softball throw. The Belizean youth tended to perform better in the pull-up, shuttle run, standing broad jump, and 600-yard run-walk.

From the statistics gathered, scores and percentiles were calculated and placed in charts that were presented in a teachers' manual. Two hundred copies of this manual were eventually printed in Belize City at the Government Printers in July 1973.

The tests may be over forty years old, but except for the 600-yard run-walk[3], which was found not to be the best for measuring endurance, the others are still considered valid as designed (bent knee adjustment may be considered in the sit-up). These tests were popular for over twenty years in the United States, where youth fitness testing is an established institution.

When the test is administered in Belize today, students can compare their scores with the established norms of their grandparents!

There are not many countries that can boast of having a youth-oriented performance test. Some that do include: United States, Canada, Poland and other European countries, Singapore, Japan, Taiwan, Australia, and Belize.

During 2012 the original fitness manual was edited and reprinted as a fortieth anniversary issue of the original publication. The 2012 edition was an unauthorized project that I undertook.

On January 1, 2013, copies were mailed to all secondary schools in Belize. Extra copies and original research material that included the original softball and shuttle blocks were mailed to the Ministry of

Education. This was all done with the hope that the material might be of some use in the current school system.[4]

Ministry of Education, Youth and Sports

My Ref: GEN/59/13(41)

11 February 2013

Mr. Ted W. Cox
Old World Deli
341 SW 2nd Street
Corvallis

Dear Mr. Cox,

I acknowledge with thanks receipt of your letter along with postal package which included the following:

20 booklets (The Physical performance Test for Belize)
1 Softball
1 DVD
2 Wooden Blocks

I take this opportunity to convey my thanks for your contribution to sports in Belize and to inform you that your work will be passed on to the National Sports Council, whom I am certain, will appreciate the literature.

Thank you once again for your thoughtfulness.

Sincerely yours,

DAVID LEACOCK
CHIEF EXECUTIVE OFFICER

173. Thank you letter from CEO David Leacock. 2013.

22
Notes

[1] In 1976, the author completed a master's thesis at Oregon State University regarding this project. *Physical Fitness Parameters of Male Youth in U.S.A. and Belize, Central America.* Submitted in partial fulfillment of the requirements for the degree of Master of Science in the School of Education.

[2] Vin Lawrence. *National Youth Programme: Youth in Belize—Moving Towards Development.* (Belize City: Government Printers, 1972), 19.

[3] Although not recognized for endurance, the 600-yard run-walk is a good measurement of an individual's speed. Today's students can compare their best time with those published in 1973.

[4] The Belize National Sports Council has a CD available of the 2013 revised Belize Fitness Manual.

23
Peace Corps
Midterm Conference

Peace Corps Belize held a mid-tour conference for my group of volunteers in order to obtain feedback and suggestions and to exchange information and relax. Since I was a more experienced volunteer, Alex Frankson asked if I would help coordinate and assist with the conference.

Letter Home
November 1, 1972
Belize City

On the weekend of October 13-15 we had our midterm conference at San Pedro, Ambergris Caye. I was the chairman. We had a good mixture of work and play. Friday at 8:40 a.m. we departed by boat moored at the Customs Office minus one volunteer – Bill Cain.

After eating lunch at the Caye, I administered an evaluation questionnaire to all the volunteers and then compiled the responses.

The reef is about ¼ mile from the village and I swam out with a friend using fins. It took a while to reach.

At 8:00 p.m. we had a general meeting.

174. San Pedro, Ambergris Caye. Peace Corps Midterm Conference. St. Peter's College. October 13-15, 1972.

175. Peace Corps Midterm Conference. Volunteer impromptu jam at Hotel Emerald Isle. October 14, 1972.

On Saturday and Sunday following our meetings, and after completing my reports, I went out on a boat with a group of Volunteers. The cost for all of us was $140 BH. It was really beautiful under the water with all kinds of colored fish and coral.

On Sunday I was on the outside of the reef trying to shoot fish with my spear gun. Lucky I'm a bad shot. After about an hour of swimming and shooting I missed one particular fish and when I looked to my left I saw a shark five to six feet long about fifteen feet from me. Remembering that sharks are drawn to blood, I lost all my desire to hunt fish, and slowly swam back to the other side of the reef and the safety of the boat.

October was a somewhat rainy month. I worked around it as best I could with my performance testing.

From November 20th to December 1st, I will be conducting a youth leaders games course sponsored by the Social Development Department. This will be held at the Belize Teachers' College.

I sent a letter to Oregon State University inquiring about graduate study but only received non-encouraging news. I also sent a letter to cousin Janet, asking her to see OSU for me and I received some encouraging news. She mailed me an application to OSU along with other necessary information. If I get offered a fellowship or assistantship I will take it. If not, I still hope to go to Eastern Illinois University.

Love, Teddy

176. *Ambergris Caye. Volunteers on the reef. October 15, 1972.*

Not long after the mid-term conference, I received word that my application to Oregon State University, in Corvallis, Oregon, had been accepted. Attending OSU eventually led to an advanced education degree in 1976. I have lived and worked in Corvallis since that time.

24
National Agricultural Show Belmopan
Developmental Competition Belize City

Since 1970 when the first National Agricultural Show was held in Belmopan, the annual event has attracted thousands of people both from all over the country and from abroad. A total of 8,000 persons attended in 1971.

The above quote was taken from the 1972 show program. Since that time the show has been run successfully for over forty years and is the largest public event held in Belize today.

The agricultural show aims to educate the public on the importance of agriculture for the future development of Belize. Some of the activities during 1972 included a rodeo, bugle band performance, crowning of Miss Agriculture, aerial spraying demo, dance, rides, display booths, and lots of food and drink. Today's, organizers estimate the event attracts over 30,000 visitors each year.

Journal
November 11, 1972 – Saturday
Belmopan

4:00 p.m. Frank Cervantes and I left Stann Creek on a bus for Belmopan to see the Agricultural Show. We stayed with Darius Martinez at his house on Oriole Street and went to a dance at the fairgrounds that night. Had quite a good time.

Journal
November 12, 1972 – Sunday
Belmopan

Spent day at the fairgrounds in Belmopan. The rain caused the area to be very muddy. Took some pictures.

Ted W. Cox

177. Belmopan. Robert Mitchell loading an exhibition basket from the Social Development Department into the ministry Land Rover. November 12, 1972.

178. Belmopan. National Agricultural Show. 1st Battalion Devon and Dorset smoke screen demonstration. November 12, 1972.

179. Soldiers running behind exhibition smoke screen. November 12, 1972.

180. Belmopan. National Agricultural Show Rodeo. November 12, 1972.

Following my weekend in Belmopan, I returned to Belize City where I assisted in a combined developmental cycle and track meet on November 14 at the National Stadium located on the north side of town.

181. Belize City. National Stadium. Bill Lightburn timing a race at Cycle and Track Developmental Meet. November 14, 1972.

182. Belize City. PCV William Kolberg and Gilmore Hinkson marking track at the National Stadium. November 14, 1972.

183. Belize City. National Stadium. Cycle and Track Developmental Meet. November 14, 1972.

184. Belize City. National Stadium. Cycle and Track Developmental Meet. Official Gilmore Hinkson. November 14, 1972.

25
Garifuna Settlement Days 1972

In November 1972, Darius Martinez invited me for a second year to celebrate Garifuna Settlement Days in Stann Creek. Stann Creek was shortly thereafter renamed Dangriga. The following pictures were taken during the trip. The first pictures are of Darius's family and friends, who I met during this visit.

Ted W. Cox

185.Stann Creek. Darius Martinez holding his daughter Gaynor. November 18, 1972.

Journal
November 18, 1972
Stann Creek

I arrived in Stann Creek at 9:30 p.m. last night. Rested today at Darius's house and visited with his parents and family. At night Darius and I went out and partied until 3:00 a.m.

Ted W. Cox

186. Stann Creek. Darius's daughter Gaynor. November 18, 1972.

187. Stann Creek. William and Lillette Flowers. November 18, 1972.

Journal
November 19, 1972
Stann Creek
 Got up at 9:00 a.m. and had breakfast. By 11 a.m. we went out and partied until 4:00 p.m.

Ted W.Cox

188. Stann Creek. This bridge spans North Stann Creek River and divides the town into Dangriga North and Dangriga South. November 19, 1972.

189. Stann Creek. Alexandrina Martinez (1903-1997). November 18, 1972.

190. Stann Creek. Clockwise, beginning with the tallest girl: Bernadette Locario, William and Lillette Flowers, Gaynor Martinez, and Lennox Flowers. November 19, 1972.

191. Stann Creek. Celebrating at Golden Bowl during Settlement Days. November 19, 1972.

192. Stann Creek. Relaxing at the Kennedy Club. Oscar Ramirez, on far left, wearing glasses. November 20, 1972.

John Canoe performers come out during the holidays to dance the Wanaragua. Historically, the John Canoe character is a masked dancer who mocked the slave owners. He danced in the neighborhood during holiday season to entertain and receive food, drink or money donations.

Ted W. Cox

193. Stann Creek. John Canoe surrounded by some intoxicated "friends" during Settlement Days. November 19, 1972.

194. Stann Creek. Miss Belmopan 1972 visiting during Settlement Days. November 19, 1972.

Journal
November 20, 1972
    Took a nap, then a bath in the ocean about 11:00 p.m.
    Got up at 6:00 a.m. By 7:30 we went to see the reenactment of the Garifuna arriving on British Honduran shores in the 19th century.

Garifuna Settlement Days celebrations began in 1941. Each year the locals reenact the 1832 arrival of the Garifuna people to Dangriga/Stann Creek. Early in the morning participants go out to the sea in boats, wait till the appointed time and then paddle to shore, waving palm fronds and banana leaves to symbolize the establishment of agriculture in their new homeland.

Ted W. Cox

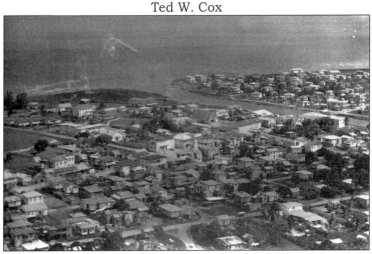

195. Stann Creek River. March 3, 1973.

196. Stann Creek. Settlement Days Reenactment. November 20, 1972.

197. Stann Creek. Reenactment of settlers paddling up Stann Creek River. November 20, 1972.

198. Stann Creek. Settlement Days Reenactment. Arrival. November 20, 1972.

199. Unloading a boat. November 20, 1972.

200. Stann Creek. Reenactment. Jerris Valentine welcoming a weary traveler. November 20, 1972.

201. *Stann* *Creek.* *Reenactment.* *Jerris Valentine helping unload. November 20, 1972.*

202. Stann Creek. Reenactment. Getting off the boat. November 20, 1972.

203. Stann Creek. Reenactment. Walking to church. November 20, 1972.

204. Stann Creek. Welcoming travelers. November 20, 1972.

205. Stann Creek. Reenactment. November 20, 1972.

206. Stann Creek. Jerris Valentine leading the drumming to church. November 20, 1972.

26
The United Nations
Christmas 1972

During the start of the 1960s the United Nations resolved that the new decade would be dedicated to helping end poverty in third world countries. Nations like British Honduras were actively casting off their colonial status and the U.N. resolved to try ending poverty as well. Experts argued that children's needs should be built into national development plans.

By the end of the decade, another hurdle fighting poverty became evident. As strides were made to improve the quality of life, so did a resulting population explosion worldwide threaten to undermine the gains that had been made. Ironically, basic modern health care improvements made the population explosion possible.

In 1966 the United Nations, through UNICEF, embraced the concept of "responsible parenthood." Family planning, a very controversial issue, was looked at in terms of promoting literacy, raising the age of marriage and avoiding unwanted pregnancies.[1]

Thus, it was in this atmosphere that during the spring of 1971 a United Nations Youth Advisor was requested by the local government of British Honduras to identify the problems confronting early school leavers and young adults, a group that represented about one-third of the Belizean population. The U.N. expert, Vin Lawrence, arrived on September 13, 1972, and I was to provide him assistance. Many organizations, social workers, citizens, youths and youth leaders collaborated on the preparation of his report. He worked for three months on the project.

Vin Lawrence wrote the final report, which was printed into a 180-page booklet entitled *National Youth Programme: Youth in Belize—Moving Towards Development.* This report was presented to the Ministry of Local Government Community and Social Development.

207. *Belize City. Vin Lawrence and Mr. Malek (on the right) supervising the printing of the report on youth in Belize at Government Printers. December 1972.*

Some of the study's findings were:

1. About 70% of Belizean youth ended their education at the primary school level. A high percentage of youth aged 14 to 25 did not have jobs.

2. The education system was unsuited to achieve the needs of the nation. It was geared too much towards academic goals, lacking in student preparation for social and economic development.

3. There were inadequate vocational facilities.

4. There was a lack of usable play fields.

5. There was a lack of voluntary youth leaders.

The study observed that large-scale unemployment tends to create an angry generation that often finds vandalism and violence the easiest ways to alleviate frustration. There were similar challenges in other developing countries of the Caribbean and the surrounding area.

Original thinking and experimentation were needed to create hope and ambition, difficult goals.

Undoubtedly, there was no single solution for bringing young people into the wage-earning mainstream. The report emphasized the need to educate Belizean youth with appropriate vocational training and to encourage interest in the agricultural potential of the country.

The study proposed a blueprint and overview of a national youth program through the year 2000. One outcome was that the government planned to establish a special youth section as part of the Social Development Department, with four basic objectives in mind:

1. To encourage interest in agriculture as a gainful occupation.
2. To reduce unemployment.
3. To raise the standard of living for young people.

4. To create an environment for young people that promotes pride in country.

When young people failed to find jobs, many understandably became anxious to migrate to the United States. At the time it was estimated that over 25,000 Belizeans were living in the United States, a large percentage considering that the entire population of the country in 1972 was only 120,000.

In a discussion I had with Terrance Jones, caretaker at MCC Grounds, he observed that a few of the individuals leaving the country were chronic troublemakers and their exit was welcomed. Unfortunately, many of these people got into trouble and were eventually sent back to Belize.

Although in the end the UN study had little to do with my assigned job, I was pleased to provide some information used in the final report.

* * * * *

Christmas in Belize has always been a very special time. Belizeans brought out their best and celebrated to the max, even if they couldn't afford to. Some went into debt and it often took months for them to bail themselves out. At Holden Hospital in Belize City, the finest linen was brought out and used, only to be stored again after the holidays.

My sister-in-law Marilyn Cox visited Belize with me during Christmas 1975 and in September 2013 commented:

Marilyn: So that was something that always stuck in my mind all these many years. It's so vivid because I've never seen anything like it in my life, men carrying a big linoleum roll over their shoulder or under their arm to their home. This wonderful old man with a beautiful Creole accent told me it was a custom to put new linoleum down at Christmas time in the middle of the living room floor and to paint chairs in the house bright colors. That's how they spruced up their house for Christmas.

On Christmas Day 1972 I left my apartment in the late morning to walk across town to visit friends, but it was hours before I arrived. Typical Belizean hospitality saw people reach out to strangers. As I was walking, a stranger sitting on the veranda of his house invited me up after a greeting from the street. Next thing I knew he was sharing his best scotch whiskey for a Christmas drink as we chatted.

This kind of hospitality was normal in Belize City during those years. Governor Posnett (1972-76) said in his memoirs years later that Belizeans were among the nicest people he met during his career, and he lived in several countries during his life. I like his point of view.

Letter Home
December 28, 1972
Belize City

Dear Mother,
  I hope you received the items from Rick Sharp O.K., and that your Christmas was good.
  Christmas Eve morning I visited different families that I know. Last week I bought some small toys and candy and filled stockings with them. I put the names of children on the socks who lived at the houses I visited. I did some drinking all day too. At midnight I went to mass at Holy Redeemer Church, then home to bed. Christmas morning I took some pictures of a family I know, then went to a good friend's house for Christmas dinner. About 4:00 p.m. I went to another house for a drink. After returning home, some other friends came over about 8:30. We had a small party until about 2:00 a.m. I got up late on the 26th and went for lunch at Frank Cervantes' house.
  Next, I went to the horse races. During the final race I put my last dollar on a horse that won and walked away with three dollars. That evening I went to Mr. Bill Lightburn's house for supper and was home in bed by 10:00 p.m.
  Today I went to the airport to help welcome a dance group from Michigan. I'm hosting one of the male dancers at my house.

It's your son,
Love, Teddy
P.S. Wish you were here for Christmas.

Horse races, held at the National Stadium three or four times a year, were a popular activity that I enjoyed several times while living in Belize.

208. Belize City. Horse races at the National Stadium. April 29, 1973.

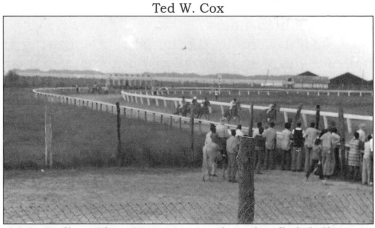

209. Belize City. Horses nearing the finish line at the National Stadium. April 29, 1973.

26
Notes

¹ "The 1960s, Decade of Development," www.unicef.org/sowc96/1960s.htm (accessed January 30, 2014).

26
Notes

¹ "The 1960s, Decade of Development," www.unicef.org/sowc96/1960s.htm (accessed January 30, 2014).

27
A Garifuna Farm

While visiting the Martinez family in November 1972, I expressed my interest to Mrs. Martinez in visiting her farm three miles from town. The following February, when I returned to conduct physical performance testing at the high schools, she asked if I was ready to make the outing and see how cassava bread is made.[1]

Journal
February 20, 1973 – Tuesday
Stann Creek

In the afternoon after testing students all day, I visited the Martinez family. Mrs. Martinez invited me to come to her farm on Thursday morning at 4:00 a.m. to see the baking of cassava bread. My answer was an immediate "yes". As we talked, I took a picture of her cousin, Mrs. Ann Noralez, who was standing nearby.

210. Stann Creek. Ann Noralez. February 20,1973.

211. Stann Creek. Domingo Martinez, Darius' father, working in his tailor shop next to their home. The shop originally was the Martinez family house. November 19, 1972.

Journal
February 21, 1973
Stann Creek

Woke up at 6:00 a.m. at the rest house. All was quiet outside. Many sand flies bothered me all night. It started raining about 7:00 a.m. with a southerly wind.

When Roy Young from the Social Development Department got up we visited. Roy and Mr. Belisle were in Stann Creek conducting a ministry sponsored conference.

He made the comment to me regarding Carib and Creole people mixing in Stann Creek. He said that about 25 years ago when there were dances in Stann Creek, they would all be separate. All Carib dances or all Creole dances. Intermarriage did not occur. But this feeling is not so strong today. With the coming of the fruit company, more Creoles came to live in Stann Creek Valley and that helped break down the cultural barrier.

When doing my official job, I stayed at the Government Rest House in Stann Creek pictured below.

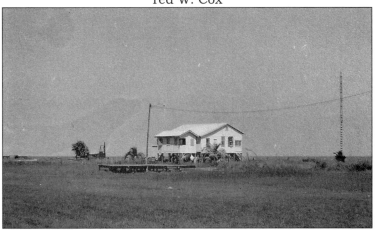

212. Stann Creek. Government Rest House. 1972.

213. Stann Creek from the 360-foot telecommunications tower. March 3, 1973.

Thursday morning arrived and I looked forward to the day's adventure.

Journal
February 22, 1973 – Thursday
Stann Creek

Got up at 4:00 a.m., dressed and went to the Martinez home. Mrs. Martinez was waiting for me. We started walking along Melinda Road for about three miles to her farm. The night was still on when we arrived. Two of her friends who I met the previous November were already preparing a fire to cook cassava inside the shelter. The area was still quite dark even though there was a partial moon out. The two women giggled when they saw me with Mrs. Martinez.

Soon the fire lit up the hut with a glow and birds were heard singing.

The farm was planted mostly in sweet cassava, bitter cassava, some medicinal plants, cashew trees, and a coconut tree.

As the large sticks in the fire were reduced to coals, they were pulled to the outside and a big round piece of sheet metal was placed on top of four iron pegs. The sheet metal pan, called the comal, was about 3 feet 6 inches in diameter. The coals heated the comal up uniformly. Next, the cassava, which had already been cleaned, grated, sieved and water squeezed out, was sprinkled onto the comal evenly. The grated cassava was patted and pressed with the hands. It cooked a little over an 1/8 of an inch thick. Steam from the cassava rose after about two minutes. The whole piece of bread became bonded and browned on the bottom side. The bread was then turned over and cooked on the other side.

The light of day soon revealed the extent of the farm. Mrs. Martinez began to prepare breakfast. She turned on her little battery-powered radio and we listened to Eddie Seferino give his wakeup call to the country (Page 58).

Ted W. Cox

214. Alexandrina Martinez preparing breakfast under shelter at her farm on Melinda Road. February 22, 1973.

215. Francisca Pais with cooked cassava bread ready for market. February 22, 1973.

I left the farm at 8:00 a.m. and was back in Stann Creek by 8:55 a.m.

Before leaving town, Mrs. Martinez asked if I was interested to see how the cassava was prepared following its harvest. She invited me to return to the farm on Thursday, March 1.

The following week I again stayed at the Government Rest House, as I was completing my work with the physical performance testing.

Thursday morning I got up at 5 a.m. and returned with Mrs. Martinez to the farm. A number of pictures show the various processes used to prepare the cassava.

When the root is first harvested, it is washed, peeled and then grated on a long mahogany board which has many rough pebbles pounded into the surface. The grated cassava is then placed in a long woven tubular strainer called the wowla, and its watery juice is pressed out. The compressed cassava is removed and is now called sebiba. This is put through a sieve and then cooked into large, thin sheets of cassava bread, as the women had done the previous week. For the Carib people, this is the most popular type of bread.

216. Martha Noralez grating cassava using a mahogany board with hard sharp stones pounded into its face. March 1, 1973.

217. Alexandrina Martinez preparing cassava bread by pressing watery juice from freshly graded cassava in woven wowla. March 1, 1973.

Crude pieces of cassava that do not go through the sieve are baked on the comal just like the bread until they become quite brown. The cooked product is then broken up and soaked in water until it ferments naturally. When the brew is ready to drink, ginger is mashed or grated and added with sugar to taste. The resulting beverage, which has some alcohol in it, is called heyou and is poured into cups or calabash to enjoy.

Bitter cassava is simply grated not cooked. A tripod is then set up to which a cloth is attached in the form of a bag. The grated cassava is then placed into the bag. A bowl, called the badaya, is placed underneath to catch the juice. The resulting juice, very toxic, is skimmed off. What is left is the starch, which is set in the sun on sheets of corrugated metal roofing to dry. The starch can then be used to make another popular Carib food, fufu.

218. Alexandrina Martinez squeezing starch from pieces of cassava through a strainer. March 1, 1973.

219. Extracting starch from chunky grated cassava. March 1, 1973.

220. Carib women planting cassava. Left to right, Francisca Pais, Mauricia Bonillo, Martha Noralez, Alexandrina Martinez. March 1, 1973.

I left the farm about 7:45 a.m., taking some homemade jam back for Mr. Martinez.

27
Notes

[1] Cassava is an edible starchy tuberous root somewhat similar to the potato. When prepared for eating, it packs a lot of calories, making it a recognized food staple for millions of people worldwide.

In Belize, there are two kinds of cassava: sweet and bitter. The sweet cassava has darker green leaves than the bitter one, and is the one from which cassava bread is made. The bitter cassava is the one from which the starch is made.

28
Testing in Punta Gorda
Return to Belize City

Journal
March 5, 1973
Punta Gorda

Flew into Punta Gorda from Stann Creek at 9:30 a.m. Upon arrival I went to see the principal of St. Peter Claver, Mr. Duran. We made last-minute adjustments to the physical performance testing schedule, and visited with Sister Ignacia, a Palatine nun in charge of the Health Clinic. She agreed to let me weigh the boys on the scale at the hospital.

I started physical performance testing at St. Peter Claver College in the afternoon with the permission of the principal, Mr. Duran.

Journal
March 6, 1973
Punta Gorda

Went to football field to administer the 600-yard run.

Francis Hecker had signed up for the track and field course in Punta Gorda that I taught in 1972. He became a friend who I visited on my second trip there.

221. Stann Creek Airport. A plane arriving from Belize City to continue on to Punta Gorda. The cost of a one-way flight to Punta Gorda was $18 B.H. March 5, 1973.

Journal
March 7, 1973
Punta Gorda

Went to see Mr. Francis Hecker around 4 p.m. He was just leaving for a BBQ party at a nearby ornamental arboretum and invited me to come along.

We drove to mile 12 on the Southern Highway and turned into an area where there was a lot of developed land. Grass was cut neatly and there were manicured trees. A retired Englishman named Mr. Wright owns the property, which he has for sale.

> The party was held in the back of the property in a clearing in the jungle with a swimming hole surrounded by cut grass and a variety of exotic trees and plants. The surroundings were delightful. There was plenty of fresh BBQ pork and Belizean rum.

Ted W. Cox

222. Punta Gorda. Francis Hecker, of the British Honduras Marketing Board, (on the right) prepares pork for a BBQ at the ornamental farm. March 7, 1973.

Journal
March 8, 1973
Belize City

   Tested last class at Peter Claver. Finished by 8:45 a.m. I walked back to Hotel Isabel and got my things ready. Francis sent his Land Rover from the Marketing Board to take me to the airstrip. Mr. Lopez and Mr. Belisle from the Ministry went with me. The plane was ready when we arrived at 9:15. We flew to Belize City with stops at Mango Creek and Stann Creek.

When arriving at my apartment in Belize City I discovered the place had been broken into on Tuesday night. The only thing that I could find stolen was a two-pound lobster that I had in my freezer.

At 4 p.m. I caught a bus to Belmopan for $1.25 B.H. I plan to help with the National 4-H Day tomorrow.

Journal
March 9, 1973
Belize City

Roy Bradley from Social Development picked me up at Darius Martinez's house in Belmopan about 9:30 a.m. We went to Forestry building to pick up hurdles to be used at the field day competition. They were not ready, so I stayed with the carpenter and we constructed 24 hurdles.

Roy returned with truck at 2:00 p.m. and I spent the afternoon helping run the 4-H Field Day at the National Agricultural Show Grounds. The day was fun but a bit unorganized.

Afterwards I caught a ride with Social Development driver Mr. Bradley back to Belize City. We arrived by 11 p.m.

Ted W. Cox

223. Belmopan. Roy Bradley loading hurdles for National 4-H Field Day. March 9, 1973.

Ted W. Cox

224. Belize City. National Stadium. Cycle race. March 11,1973.

337

225. MCC Grounds. Manfred Atkins announcing on Radio Belize; Bill Lightburn (in hat) taking notes. March 11, 1973.

Journal
March 11, 1973
Belize City

Went to cycle races at the National Stadium. I helped with time-keeping and took some pictures. Later I went to the MCC Grounds and took a picture of Mr. Lightburn record-keeping and Manfred Atkins announcing at an inter-district knock-out football game. Orange Walk vs. Stann Creek.

226. *MCC Grounds. Minister of Sports, Louis Sylvestre, congratulates a member of the winning Orange Walk team. Manfred Atkins interviews him live on Radio Belize. March 11, 1973.*

29
To San Pedro
for Testing and Fun

St. Peter's College (a high school), was founded in 1971 by Frank Nunez, the school's first principal. At that time San Pedro, located on the island of Ambergris Caye, was a bustling village of just under 1,000 that sported a multi-million-dollar commercial fisheries industry. High school classes had been held in the Community Center. There were only twenty-five first form students at the time of testing in 1972.

Considerable financial assistance making this school possible came from some Americans living in Wisconsin. These Americans had originally met Frank Nunez when visiting the caye on a vacation.

The dates I was scheduled to visit and conduct physical performance testing were originally set for March 11-16.

Journal
March 13, 1973
Belize City

Sent a telegram to Mr. Frank Nunez (principal, St. Peter's College) that I was coming that night to San Pedro to start the physical fitness testing next day.

Rick Sharp came along to assist me. We left Belize City on the cargo boat *Emma* at 6:30 p.m. with a full load of kerosene and soft drinks. The weather was not bad, but there was only a half moon out. This made it a bit dark and navigation was difficult for the captain. We kept inside the reef all the way, a passage filled with hazards from shallows and numerous coral heads. We reached San Pedro 12:30 at night.

Rick wanted to get accommodations, but the village was asleep, so we slept on the boat.

Ted W. Cox

227. *San Pedro, Ambergris Caye. Rick Sharp stands on* Emma *cabin roof after waking up. March 13, 1973.*

We got up at 6:00 a.m. Some fishermen were already fishing. We walked toward the high school and stopped by one house to ask where Mr. Nunez lived. The neighbor pointed us in the right direction and we found him standing in the doorway of the general store across the lane from his house. He had not received the message I sent from Belize City. Mr. Nunez took me to meet the village chairman, Mr. Enrique Staines, and made arrangements for our breakfast. Afterwards we went to the health clinic and arranged to weigh the children with the help of the nurse. Next we walked to the high school and made testing arrangements. We also met with Mr. Reyes, the principal of San Pedro Roman Catholic Primary School.

We then went for an outing with Mr. Nunez and Mr. Staines on what they called the lagoon route behind the town. Staines was very nice to us and gave a thrilling ride through six miles of mangrove. We cut in and out of waterways that were very narrow.

Ted W. Cox

228. We darted through mangrove swamp behind San Pedro, Ambergris Caye, on the way to Mr. Robinson's lodge. March 16, 1973.

Our first stop was at Mr. Robinson's lodge. Robinson is an agent for Bucknor Shipping Line, and Mr. Staines is one of the caretakers for the lodge. While there, we went swimming on the reef. Later, about noon, we visited an ocean trap to see if there were any fish. Mr. Staines man-handled a large sea turtle into the boat, and then speared a four-foot barracuda. The barracuda broke away from the line. I did not know it was a barracuda and jumped into the trap to look for it. Damn glad I didn't find it. Mr. Staines caught it and brought it into the boat. Its teeth looked mean.

We returned home and after lunch Rick and I started to administer the physical performance testing at the high school.

Journal
March 14,1973
San Pedro

Rick and I tested students at the high school football field. Minister Louis Sylvestre visited while we were there. He flew in from Belize City, politicking to get support for a bill to change the official name of the country from British Honduras to Belize.

That evening Rick, Frank and I played monopoly at Mr. Staines' house from about 9:30 p.m. to 11:45 p.m. The wind was blowing hard all day and night. I could hear the roar of waves crashing on the reef about ½ mile from shore.

Rick and I slept in the school building each night and had meals with the Staines family.

229. Ambergris Caye. Enrique Staines, San Pedro village chairman, displaying a barracuda caught in a fish trap. March 13, 1973.

Journal
March 15, 1973
San Pedro

Something that took me a while to figure out and think about was that students wear their uniform to school in the morning, looking sharp, but in the afternoons they come back to school barefooted, looking informal but comfortable. Most of the people here go barefooted. Sand is everywhere in the village. So now I'm barefooted.

We finished testing for the day and took some pictures. Rick spent some time with boys playing volleyball and I coached the girls playing softball.

Ted W. Cox

230. Ambergris Caye. St. Peter's College students playing softball. March 16, 1973.

Later at Mr. Staines' house we played monopoly and drank rum. I accidentally broke two glasses. One by my elbow and the other by my foot. Mrs. Elvi Staines gave a good-natured laugh, but I felt kind of funny. She cooked the turtle her husband caught the other day for lunch and dinner. It was very tasty. Something like tender beef but different.

Journal
March 16, 1973
San Pedro

Rick and I spent the morning at the high school. After the last class Frank had the students sing for us. As I looked out the classroom window at the reef and clear blue sea while the children sang I was thankful for such a nice gesture.

After lunch Mr. Staines took Rick, Frank and me to the lagoon behind town to bird hunt. We traveled to Mr. Robinson's lodge in the boat. The mangrove swamp was all around us. We saw an open area where the water was about 10 feet deep. It looked as though a current was gushing upwards in one spot. The water was not a flow like a river would make going into a lake. Upon moving the boat over the area, we saw a hole on the bottom about five feet by three feet. Apparently the tide from the sea was coming up through the opening. We saw two fish about three feet long swim out of the hole. Frank said at times the hole sucks water. As we came upon a mangrove island about 50 yards across, we saw many nests belonging to the cuca bird. We got off the boat and carefully walked on the mangrove, which was very swampy. A bad step could send your foot crashing through the mangrove. We killed six cuca birds.[1]

The next morning we flew to Belize City at 7:30 a.m.

231. Hunting at San Pedro, Ambergris Caye. Enrique Staines, Rick Sharp, Frank Nunez. March 16, 1973.

29
Notes

[1] In Picture 231, the birds we killed appear to be Boat-billed Herons and not cuca birds.

30
Regional and National Track and Field Competitions 1973

March and April 1973 were busy with track and field meets held all over the country, at both elementary and high schools. On March 22, I traveled from Belize City to Orange Walk to assist with the Northern Divisional Inter-Secondary School Track Meet. The bus ticket cost 65 cents U.S. The initial meeting to organize this competition was held in Orange Walk on February 2. Upon arrival, I immediately inspected the field and saw there had been a lot of work done by the staff. The field was ready and well laid out.

Letter Home
April 2, 1973
Belize City

Dear Mother,
I was in Orange Walk March 23. The high schools from Corozal came down to Orange Walk to participate in a three-way track and field meet with Muffles College. The meet was well organized. The Sisters at Muffles College let me sleep in the convent in the principal's office. I really enjoy the nuns' hospitality. In fact, the Catholic Church really has impressed me these past two years. The Fathers and Sisters are all friendly, dedicated

and helpful. I can only think of one priest in the country that was hard to work with.
Love to all, Teddy

Ted W. Cox

232. Orange Walk. Northern Divisional Inter-Secondary School Track Meet. Sister Leona, principal, Muffles College (190 high school students in 1973). March 23, 1973.

233. Orange Walk. Northern Divisional Track Meet. Judges and guest stand. March 23, 1973.

234. Orange Walk. Northern Divisional Track Meet. Plotting relay lanes. March 23, 1973.

Ted W. Cox

235. Orange Walk. Northern Divisional Track Meet. Honored guests. March 23, 1973.

236. Orange Walk. Northern Divisional Track Meet. March 23, 1973.

Ted W. Cox

237. Orange Walk. Northern Divisional Track Meet. Relay hand-off. March 23, 1973.

Ted W. Cox

238. Orange Walk. Northern Divisional Track Meet. Perfect hand-off. March 23, 1973.

239. Orange Walk. Northern Divisional Track Meet. High jump. March 23, 1973.

240. Orange Walk. Northern Divisional Track Meet. Distance run. March 23, 1973.

Ted W. Cox

241. Orange Walk. Northern Divisional Track Meet. Distance run. March 23, 1973.

Ted W. Cox

242. Orange Walk. Northern Divisional Track Meet. Fletcher College, overall champion. March 23, 1973.

243. Orange Walk. Fletcher College (high school) representative, on the left, accepts championship award from Xavier principal, Wilfredo "Fido" Aguilar. March 23, 1973.

Journal
March 20, 1973
Belize City

Spent last two days preparing the MCC Grounds for the upcoming Eastern Divisional Track and Field Meet on March 24 involving Belize City schools.

The day following the Northern Divisional Track Meet I quickly returned to Belize City to help run the Eastern Divisional Track Meet on Saturday, March 24. There was a large crowd to witness some good performances.

244. Belize City. Eastern Divisional Track Meet. Start of the 100-meter race. March 24, 1973.

245. Belize City. Eastern Divisional Track Meet.
March 24, 1973.

246. Belize City. Eastern Divisional Track Meet.
March 24, 1973.

247. Belize City. Eastern Divisional Track Meet. Albert Lovell taking an injured athlete to the first aid station. March 24, 1973.

The Southern Divisional Track Meet scheduled for March 31 in Stann Creek was postponed until April 4.

On Monday, April 2, I took a bus from Belize City to Stann Creek. The ticket cost $1.25 U.S. Another two seats were purchased for $2.50 U.S. so I could transport the wet line-marking machine.

Ned Pitts, with the help of some students, marked the field. For a second year Punta Gorda was not able to take part in this meet between Austin High and Stann Creek High.

248. Stann Creek. Meet organizer Ned Pitts, second from left, supervises the field marking at Austin High School. April 3, 1973.

* * * * *

After the success of the first National Secondary School Track Meet, described in Chapter 10, the second one was scheduled to take place on April 7, 1973, at the MCC Grounds in Belize City. Arrangements had been made to accommodate athletes arriving from the districts, starting April 5.

At the same time the visiting athletes were registered for their respective events.

For a second year, the meet was a big success - with Belize City dominating the event. Afterward, a suggestion was put forward to organizers that Belize City schools be divided into both a north and south side to give all districts an even chance to win trophies. It was difficult for the smaller rural districts to compete against the larger population of students found in Belize City.

Unfortunately, I do not have pictures of this second national track meet.

31
Stann Creek and San Ignacio Inter-Primary School Field Days

The week of April 9-13, 1973, was scheduled for Inter-Primary School Field Days in San Ignacio and Stann Creek. Primary school teachers in both districts had organized these events. Now was the time to make things happen. Fortunately for me, the field days were scheduled on different days. This gave me time to help set up and attend both activities.

In early April I participated in a meeting in Stann Creek with the organizing committee and suggested some ideas to help the event run more smoothly.

Journal
April 10, 1973 – Tuesday
San Ignacio

At 7:15 a.m., Sgt. Bill Hodgson came from Airport Camp and picked me up by the Belize City courthouse. We traveled to Camp Holdfast near Central Farm and had lunch in the sergeants' mess. Good food. There are about 140 men stationed there. We left camp at 2:00 p.m. for San Ignacio to help set up and run the Inter-Primary School Field Day scheduled for Friday. The field day is organized by the Cayo Primary School Athletic Association (CAPSAA).

249. San Ignacio. Hernan Ochaeta and Irish Guard Sgt. Bill Hodgson supervise children in marking lanes with white lime for the upcoming Inter-Primary School Field Day on April 13. April 11, 1973.

Journal
April 11, 1973 – Wednesday
San Ignacio

Bill Hodgson and I went to the district officer's house in San Ignacio at 8:45 a.m. There we met the district officer, Mr. Waight, and Hernan Ochaeta. We left with a number of children to the field to prepare it for the field day on Friday.

After lunch in San Ignacio, I saw Mr. Mitchell from the Social Development Office. He was taking Education Minister Authors to Belmopan, and I was able to catch a ride with them. From Belmopan I took another transport to Stann Creek. Upon arrival I immediately made arrangements to start work on the playing field the following morning at 5:00 a.m. The field day was scheduled to start at 11 a.m.

250. San Ignacio. Hernan Ochaeta places lane marker for the upcoming field day. April 11, 1973.

Journal
April 12, 1973 – Thursday
Stann Creek

Darius's father and I wanted to begin marking the field by 5:30 but heavy rain made our work next to impossible. This continued until 10 a.m. Panic started to settle in when I realized that we did not have enough marking powder for the athletic field.

We did note that the sandy beach lay just yards away from the proposed track. Eventually reinforcements showed up and we decided to mark the field with buckets of sand. This turned out to be a good idea. A truck was quickly filled with sufficient sand and brought close to the field.

The competition got underway and ran smoothly. Schools taking part in the Stann Creek Inter-Primary School Field Day included:

Methodist	Holy Angel
Sacred Heart	St. Matthew's
Holy Ghost	Hopkins

Ted W. Cox

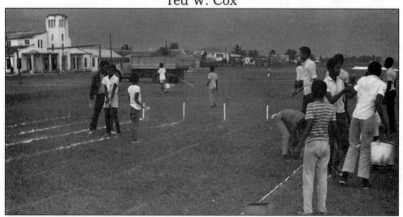

251. *Stann Creek. Filling buckets with sand from a truck to mark the running lanes. April 12, 1972.*

252. *Stann Creek. Plenty of help laying sand to indicate the running lanes. April 12, 1973.*

253. Stann Creek. Six schools took part in the Inter-Primary School Field Day. April 12, 1973.

254. Stann Creek. Inter-Primary School Field Day. April 12, 1973.

255. Stann Creek. Inter-Primary School Field Day. April 12, 1973.

Social Development driver Mitchell came by to pick me up at noon for the trip back to San Ignacio. The Stann Creek track meet was going to run late, so I had to pass up the ride. Ned Pitts said not to worry, and promised that I would be back in San Ignacio that evening. Pitts and I left Stann Creek at 5:00 p.m., heading for Roaring Creek, near Belmopan, where he dropped me off. There, I was able to catch a transfer ride to San Ignacio and arrived there about 10 p.m.

PCV Rick Sharp was already at the San Ignacio Government Rest House where we slept.

Journal
April 13, 1973
San Ignacio

By early morning everything was in place for the second annual Inter-Primary School Field Day in San Ignacio. The event was organized by the Cayo Primary School Athletic Association (CAPSAA). In addition to Cayo District teachers, B.H.A.A.A. President Norrin O. Meighan, PCV Rick Sharp, PCV Chris Dixon and British Army Sergeant Bill Hodgson were there to assist running the meet.

Ten primary schools from around the district took part:

> Unitedville
> Benque Nazarene
> Santa Elena
> Benque Roman Catholic
> San Antonio
> Cristo Ray
> Sacred Heart
> St. Andrew's
> St. Francis
> St. Barnabas

256. San Ignacio. Left to right: PCV Rick Sharp, BHAAA President Norrin O. Meighan, and the author. This picture was taken in front of Government Rest House. Hawkesworth Bridge can be seen in the background. April 13, 1973.

257. San Ignacio.
Ribbons were given to
winners of the various
competitions. April 13,
1973.

258. San Ignacio. PCV
Chris Dixon prepares
girls for the three-
legged race. April 13,
1973.

259. San Ignacio. This competitor takes the egg challenge seriously. The egg is balanced on the end of the spoon that she is holding between her teeth. April 13, 1973.

260. San Ignacio. Record keepers at the field day scoring table. April 13, 1973.

261. San Ignacio. Relay hand-off. April 13, 1973.

262. San Ignacio. Teamwork. April 13, 1973.

263. San Ignacio. Signing into competition. April 13, 1973.

264. San Ignacio. Getting ready for the sprint. April 13, 1973.

Journal
April 14, 1973
San Ignacio

The day was a big success. After ribbons were handed out and the final ceremony was completed, Rick went on his way and Bill Hodgson took me to Holdfast Camp where I spent the night. Bill and I returned to San Ignacio in the morning to measure the football field at Western High School and placed permanent markers for laying out a track in the future. We then returned to Holdfast Camp and after lunch took army transport back to Belize City.

32
Triangular Track and Field Meet, 1973

The 1973 Triangular Track and Field Meet was scheduled for May 13. This year, it was the Irish Guards who fielded the battalion team. This was the last time that this competition would be held in British Honduras. Two weeks later, the country was officially renamed Belize.

Ted W. Cox

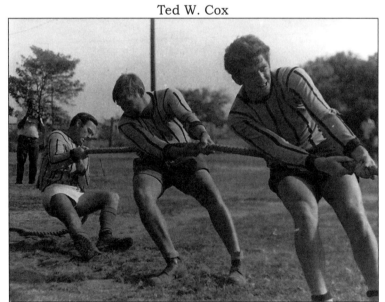

265. *Belize City. MCC Grounds. Triangular Track Meet. 1st Battalion Irish Guards competing in tug of war. May 13, 1973.*

266. Belize City. Triangular Track Meet starter Irish Guard Sgt. Bill Hodgson. May 13, 1973.

267. *Belize City. Opening ceremonies. May 13, 1973.*

268. Belize City. BHAAA competitor in the javelin throw. May 13, 1973.

269. Belize City. BHAAA competitor in the high jump. May 13, 1973.

Rob Thurston

270. Belize City. Irish Guard competitor. May 13, 1973.

Ted W. Cox

271. Belize City. Bruce Bowing throwing discus for BHAAA. May 13, 1973.

*272. Belize City. Bruce Bowing putting the shot
for BHAAA. May 13, 1973.*

273. Belize City. Eric Waight starting the medley relay. May 13, 1973.

274. Belize City. Chadwich Usher from Stann Creek running his leg of the medley relay for the BHAAA. May 13, 1973.

275. *Belize City. Albert Lovell coaches the muscle men of Belize City representing the BHAAA. May 13,1973.*

276. *Belize City. Volunteer Guard team. May 13, 1973.*

277. Belize City. 1ˢᵗ Battalion Irish Guards competing in tug of war. Bill Lightburn (white hat in back) is leaning into the pull with the guards. May 13, 1973.

278. Belize City. Triangular Track Meet.
Ted W. Cox taking a picture of Rob Thurston taking a picture of Ted. May 13, 1973.

.

Letter Home
May 17, 1973
Belize City

Dear Mother,

This past Sunday was the last track and field meet that I'll be coordinating as a Peace Corps Volunteer in British Honduras. It involved the British Army vs Belize Volunteer Guards vs the Amateur Athletic Association.

I started working on my physical fitness statistics this week. Neal Hammond is teaching me standard deviation and the basics in calculating the results. Looks like a two-week job. I have a favor to ask of Janis and Ed. The Belizean man to whom I've been directly responsible to for the last two years, Mr. Carl Coleman, will be traveling with his family to San Francisco via bus about the second week in July. I would appreciate if you would put them up for a day or two. I don't think any of them have been to the States before, and this would be a rest stop to San Francisco.
It's me, Teddy.

33
Hosting the Rowdy Texans

During 1969, Belizean Brian Roe organized a rugby club in Belize City. The main opponents over the years were the various British Army regiments stationed in Belize. During the mid-1970s the team also attended tournaments in Mexico City.

Plans were made in February 1973 to host the Houston United Athletic Club in May. The Belize Rugby Club was responsible for housing twenty of the athletes. Competitions took place in football (soccer), basketball and rugby.

I was first introduced to the game of rugby when serving in Sierra Leone in 1970. Belizean friend Dave Anderson invited me to play for the Belize Rugby Club in 1972. I took part in over a dozen games against various army regiments (and the rowdy Texans) during my stay in Belize.

On May 19, 1973, we played the Houston team at the Belize Estate and Produce Company Grounds located on Freetown Road. The Americans had good athletes, better than our side. Some of them were semi-pro American football players. Fortunately for Belize, the Americans were not acclimated to the tropical humidity, so even though they were bigger and better, they got tired quicker and didn't totally clobber us.

During the match, some of the soldiers on the sidelines made the mistake of boasting how the army would give the Yanks a hard time the next day. The Texans didn't take the comments lightly.

The army team was made up of a combination of guys from different units, and not as strong as some regiments we had played against in the past.

On Sunday the Houston team came on the field at Airport Camp with a vengeance. The Brits received quite a beating, with at least one broken nose.

Fellow Belizean teammate Dave Anderson and I reminisced about the party our team hosted for Houston the previous day, at the old Pickwick Club, following our match.

Dave: That was when we got kicked out of the old Pickwick Club, which was a private membership social club located on North Front Street, near the Eden Cinema. We were able to get in because Brian Roe was a member.

One of the Houston players, the hooker, was a big heavyset guy. He danced when we sang the tune "Zulu Warrior" as though it was a strip dance.

I cuma zimba zimba zia
I cuma zimba zimba zee
I cuma zimba zimba
I cuma zimba zimba zee
Hold them down, you Zulu warrior,
Hold them down, you Zulu chief, chief, chief.

And while we were singing the song, that fool from Houston was stripping. The thing was, all of the club members' wives who were there had their eyes glued to this bloody dancer.

When he tried to get up on a table swinging his underwear, that's when management kicked us out and told us not to come back.

While visiting in December 1975, I played for Belize in a tournament at Airport Camp.

Ted W. Cox

279. Airport Camp. Belize Team, seven-a-side rugby tournament. Left to right: Fred Garcia, William (Billy) Skeen, Dave Anderson, the author, Randolph Johnson, Rudy Gentle, Adrian Roe. December 1975.

Fred Garcia was a phlebotomist at the government lab in Belize City. Billy Skeen, on at least one occasion, jogged from Belize City to the Airport Camp before competing. Dave Anderson worked as an insurance inspector for the Belize Insurance Center in Belize City. Randolph Johnson taught high school in Belize City. Rudy Gentle was a Sgt. Major (WO2) in the Belize Defense Force. Adrian Roe, brother of club founder Brian Roe, was manager of the Caribbean Tobacco Company in Belize City.

34
When British Honduras
Became Belize
My Farewell

Premier George Price chose June 1, 1973, as the day to officially change the name of British Honduras to Belize. After almost ninety years, the time had come to shake off British Honduras, the name that represented imperial control of the territory. Belizean politicians were at the helm of guiding their country toward independence. The name change represented one of the steps in that direction.

Prior to the event, a bill approving the new name had to pass through the legislature in Belmopan. Politicians visited their various constituencies to inform voters of the plan, which had widespread support.

People were already used to the name Belize, since that was the name of the largest city. I was in San Pedro conducting physical fitness testing on March 13 when Louis Sylvestre arrived to inform his voter base there.

On May 31, Radio Belize did its part to celebrate the day, playing popular Belizean music. The night passed relatively low key for such an historical moment. Belize emerged proud but humble with neither parades nor other big celebrations. That party would have to wait eight more years until Independence Day, September 21, 1981.

As the country moved forward, I knew that I would soon be moving on also. My acceptance at Oregon State University in Corvallis, which came through in late 1972, was the next step for me to take.

Letter home
June 26, 1973
Belize City

Dear Mother and Family,

I received your last letter yesterday. Things are starting to gear down here. The weather has been hot and humid. Rain should come anytime though.

My official termination date is set for July 20th, but after that I will join the Peace Corps staff to work with the incoming trainees until August 11th.

Oregon State University offered me a half assistantship. That means I'll be pinching my money, but I decided not to let that stop me. I've sent the deposit for room and board to the Oregon State campus for adult housing in Snell Hall.

School starts September 20 in Corvallis, Oregon. I plan to spend some time with you in California and buy some sort of car before heading north.

> By the way, in case you weren't aware, British Honduras had an official name change on June 1st. The country is now officially called Belize.
>
> Love, Teddy

My last day in Belize was August 18, 1973. Bags were packed as I went to the Airport Camp ready to play one last rugby game. We won 21 to 16. This was the first time we beat the Brits during my two years in Belize!

Afterwards, friends walked over to the airport to see me off. By 7 p.m. I was on a jet flying home to the States!

Ted W. Cox

280. Airport Camp. Belize City vs. British Army. The picture shows me catching the football. August 18, 1973.

281. Airport Camp. Soldiers relaxing on the sidelines during the rugby match. In the barracks pictured, housing for the corporals and privates, we changed into our rugby gear. August 18, 1973.

282. Belize International Airport. Friend and athlete Rivero saying goodbye. Two hours following the rugby match I left for California via New Orleans. August 18, 1973.

BRITISH HONDURAS

DRIVING
PERMIT

35
Epilogue

Soon after checking into Oregon State University during the fall of 1973, I was hired to coach the university women's volleyball team. A number of good athletes were returning for what became a successful season. 1973 was the first year that a new federal law, known as Title 9, began to be implemented at OSU. Title 9 paved the way for women to have equal opportunity with men in collegiate athletic programs with federal funding.

Before classes started, I received the following letter from Gilmore Hinkson. It came in the stamped envelope pictured on the bottom of the front cover of this book:

8th September 1973
Belize City

Hello Ted,

Thanks for your letter and check of $46 and $10 U.S. for the raffle.

I do hope that you are happy at your new home.

The track shoes you sent to Rivero were delivered to him today. The medals for the Ministry and B.A.A.A. arrived on Monday 3rd September 1973 and both prizes got here in due time, thanks

---

to your personal efforts. I also notice you sold a book of raffle tickets to the firm of Trophy King Awards in Pomona, California. I hope that you will be successful at your new area.

Due to the wet conditions of the MCC Grounds, the athletic meet had to postpone until Saturday 15th September 1973. The competitors are fair enough. The army entered two competitors for each track and three for field events. This will be an interesting track meet.

Hoping all is well with you. So long until a next time.

Gilly Hinkson

I planned to fly back to Belize for the Christmas break. On December 13, I drove 900 miles from Corvallis to Ontario, California, arriving early the next morning. About 11:15 a.m. my brother-in-law Ed drove me to the Los Angeles International Airport. After some lengthy delays, I arrived in New Orleans at 8:30 a.m. on the 15.

The flight from New Orleans to Belize departed at 9:00 a.m. My seat was in the tail section. Almost all of the passengers were from Latin America. One man sitting directly across from me was intoxicated and a bit loud and cocky. For some reason, he did not fasten his seat belt.

Upon takeoff we immediately flew into a violent thunderstorm and the aircraft began bouncing around. The man without the seat belt was tossed out of his seat and began to panic, so I unbuckled myself and reached out to him. After pushing him back and securing his seatbelt, I found the return to my seat even more challenging. Most people were holding hands across the aisles and praying out loud in Spanish. At some point, lightning hit the aircraft, and that's when I started to get scared. Eventually the storm abated and the flight continued.

At the Belize Airport, I saw Gilmore Hinkson dropping off a friend. Hinkson said that there was a track meet at the MCC Grounds and took me there. I timed some races and officiated the high jump. The day was sunny and warm. Afterwards I walked over to Rick Sharp's house, which happened to be my old apartment. Then I dropped my belongings off at Frank Cervantes' house and went with PCV Tarmo Jaagus to PCV Tad Marx's house on Regent Street. We partied until 5:00 a.m.

283. Belize City. PCV Rick Sharp, on left, officiating Developmental Track Meet at the MCC Grounds. December 15, 1973.

Journal
December 16, 1973 – Sunday
Belize City

Got up at 5:00 a.m. at Tad's and started for Frank Cervantes' house on Victoria Street. As I passed by Holy Redeemer Church I noticed that people were entering, so I went in for the 5:30 Mass. When I was leaving, Premier George Price was right behind me. I was not aware of him until a man on a bicycle passed by and said, "Morning, Sir," and the Premier answered: "Good morning, mon."

At Frank's parents' house I slept until noon and then visited with the family. After taking a shower, I noticed a small Listerine mouthwash bottle in the medicine cabinet. I opened the bottle and took some to gargle. But there was a big surprise. The taste was terrible and I immediately spit the contents into the sink. I found out later that Frank's dad had filled the bottle with marijuana soaked in white rum. Mr. Cervantes used the potion as a rub to ease the pain on his arthritic joints.

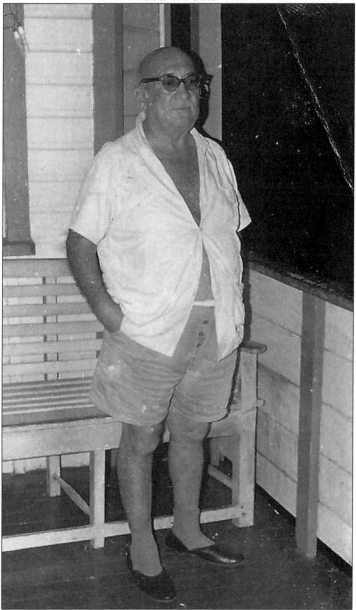

284. Belize City. Francisco Cervantes, Frank's father, on the veranda of his house on Victoria Street. 1973.

During the four months since I had left Belize, I had looked into the possibility of returning one day to establish an outdoor school near Belize City. I felt that urban children needed to have an educational experience in a rural setting. There, children could study nature firsthand and play sports. Bill Lightburn and I had already discussed the idea and he embraced the plan wholeheartedly.

Journal
December 17, 1973 – Monday
Belize City

I found out that Norrin O. Meighan was traveling to Cayo District. He was kind enough to give me a ride to Belmopan where I visited with the Ministry of Local Government staff and had a conversation with Carl Coleman regarding establishing an outdoor school in Belize.

285. Belize City. Bill Lightburn in his house on Euphrates Ave. October 2, 1972.

Journal
December 18, 1973
Belize City

Went for a visit to Bill Lightburn's house on Euphrates Avenue. He is currently taking care of twelve children in his home. There were also two ladies present who were related to him.

I was not surprised when two mice came out to nibble some food we dropped by our feet in the dining room. Bill said they didn't hurt anything, "so let them be," and we continued our conversation. He shared some homemade rum po-po.

One lady in the house named Auntie told me that Creole women sometimes rub coconut fat on their legs to make hair grow. She suggested I use some on my balding head.

After lunch I went to the Peace Corps Office and talked for a while with Director Alex Frankson.

Then I was off to Holden Memorial Hospital to see Juanita, Rob Thurston's wife. She just had a baby girl on Sunday. While in her hospital room I looked out the window and thought how pretty the view of the sea was. I left the hospital by 5 p.m. and walked over to Norman's. On my way I saw Leni Jo Usher driving by on Albert Street. Talked to her for a minute. Roy Leslie drove by, I got into his car, and he drove me for a drink at Queen Anne. We went through ½ quart of Appleton rum. Had a good talk. He had just gotten back from a workshop week in Jamaica.

That night Frank Cervantes, Jaime Sanchez and I went to see a movie.

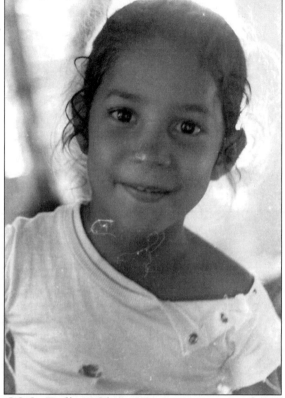

286. Belize City. Maureen, one of Bill Lightburn's grandchildren. November 1972.

During my visit to Bill's home, he mentioned owning property on the Belize River that might be appropriate for the outdoor school. The land was located about twenty miles from Belize City. Bill eventually gave me an informal deed to three acres of the property.

287. *Informal deed to three acres near Little Falls.*
1973.

> *Due to our mutual interest in athletics, and the*
> *friendship evolving therefrom, I William Lightburn*
> *hereby deed to Ted Cox three acres of my land*
> *situated at Little Falls, right bank ascending the*
> *Belize River. This land will enable him to develop a*
> *summer camp for the further benefit of the young*
> *people of Belize to whom he has given several years*
> *of athletic coaching, which improved the prowess of*
> *secondary schools in the entire country.*
> *W. Lightburn.*

My idea was to build a facility that
initially focused on city children in the fifth
and sixth grades. For a week in a rural
setting they would learn about forest, river,
plant and animal life from trained

413

instructors. During the week, the children's classroom teacher would supervise and be involved.

Bill loved to see children given opportunities of all kinds, and this project was dear to him.

During 1978, the plan received some local press in Corvallis:

> Last January, Cox returned to Belize to inspect three acres of land, which had been given to him on which to establish an outdoor school and sports center for children. He said the donor of the land was a Belize native, William Lightburn, 72, who heads a large family.[1]

Empirical evidence in the United States indicated that children tended to develop a closer bond with their teachers after taking part in this type of experience.

By 1979, I had made three trips to Belize, presenting the plan to administrators, teachers, and interested citizens. A second news article from Oregon shows that for me the project was still alive in 1979.

> Belizeans are very interested in providing an outdoor educational opportunity for urban kids and I'll be returning around Easter to give a presentation on how the school can be run and the different problems I see.[2]

Unfortunately, by 1981 the project came to a halt, as I felt the need to choose between my restaurant business in Corvallis, Oregon, or making a 100% commitment to Belize. The problem facing me at the time was how to raise capital for the outdoor school. Today, I realize finances were not an obstacle. With an endorsement from the Belizean government and a well-written plan of action, I am sure that corporate sponsors would have come forward.

So, an unforgettable and extremely rewarding chapter in my life came to a close. There is satisfaction in knowing that athletes and leaders can, and do, work together for their nation's sporting excellence. My experience taught me that, with imagination and good planning, great things can happen in Belize.

35
Notes

[1] "Aid sought for storm-torn nation," *Corvallis Gazette Times* (Corvallis, Oregon), October 5, 1978.
[2] "Outdoor school dream nears reality," *Benton Bulletin* (Philomath, Oregon), November 28, 1979.

PROGRESS REPORT THREE

Official Report to Ministry of Local Government
June 1972

To: Honorable Louis Sylvestre
    Ministry of Local Government, Community &
    Social Development
From: Director/Coach for Track and Field

This report is organized into the following sections:
1. National Track and Field Course
2. Athletic Meetings
3. Equipment Inventory
4. National Records
5. Expansion of program
6. Training of Dorla Flowers
7. Counter Part
8. Proposed Projects

1.   NATIONAL TRACK AND FIELD COURSE

During the month of December 1971, I made introductory visits to each of the district towns except Punta Gorda, to arrange for conducting the National Coaches Clinic. In January and February, a rigid schedule was followed in which approximately sixty-one persons in the districts successfully completed the course. These people were introduced to organizing, conducting, officiating, and coaching various events of Track and Field.

417

Track Clinic Schedule
1972

Date	Location
January 3–16	San Ignacio
January 10–24	Belmopan
January 27–31	Orange Walk
February 1-9	Corozal
February 11-26	Stann Creek
February 18-23	Punta Gorda

In addition to this schedule, from January to May I taught the same material at the Belize Teachers College, Belize City, where I gave instruction to Physical Education elective students.

The Track and Field course was a success, stimulating recent district activities on both the primary and secondary school level.

2.   ATHLETIC MEETINGS

SECONDARY SCHOOLS

Interest was expressed to me from the time of my arrival in August 1971, to involve the country in a national high school athletic event.

After a conversation with Mr. Ned Pitts, plans were laid for the Amateur Athletic Association (with the cooperation from the Ministry of Education), to organize the country into sections. Each section would conduct their own divisional track and field meets, with the best athletes coming to Belize City for a national track and field meet.

418

I was able to hold meetings with all secondary school principals in the country, to present the plan.

From these efforts, for the first time in British Honduras, track and field meets were held in all areas of the country to select the best athletes for participation in a national secondary school meet.

March 4, 1972	Belize City
March 24, 1972	Belmopan
April 14, 1972	Corozal, Orange Walk
April 15, 1972	Stann Creek
April 22, 1972	National Secondary Schools Track Meet

PRIMARY SCHOOLS

San Ignacio – March 24, 1972:

From the time I first conducted the Track and Field Course in San Ignacio, the Primary School Teachers Union of San Ignacio expressed interest to organize a field day for the primary schools in their town. One man who had taken the track and field course was a key organizer of this event. I was invited to attend these meetings and helped conduct the First Annual Track and Field Day for San Ignacio Primary Schools held on Friday, March 24th, 1972. Plans are being made to include schools from the entire district next year.

Yo Creek – May 23, 1972:

The Teachers' Union of Orange Walk organized a district primary school track and field meet, which was held in Yo Creek on May 23rd,1972.

Two men who took the track and field course in Orange Walk were key organizers of this event.

Ten schools took part from the district.

Triangular Track and Field Meet – June 11, 1972

Plans to revive the triangular track meet were first discussed last November with representatives of the Amateur Athletic Association, Police and British Army. The date had to be postponed from April 1st to June 11th due to unavoidable problems.

The MCC Grounds benefited from the assistance the Army gave in providing certain equipment and preparing the grounds.

3.   EQUIPMENT INVENTORY

On Saturday May 27th, 1972 the Peace Corps Office on Daly Street was broken into. Among the items stolen were four Han Hart stop watches, which were the property of the Ministry of Local Government. The matter was reported to the police.

On June 8th, 1972 one of the new cross bars was broken during the Army Battalion sports meeting.

4.   NATIONAL RECORDS

Record keeping for Track and Field has not been secure. The problem of organizing past records by Belizean athletes is a difficult one, especially when accuracy is of prime importance. Mr. William Lightburn has been of great assistance in regards to athletic history. From him I have borrowed records, which he has kept over the years. They were returned after sorting for his editing. He has been researching old newspapers to compare and bring the records up to date. Presently, Mr. Lightburn has chronicled records starting from 1902 in certain events. These efforts will prove to be of historical significance for the country.

Standards should be put in place under which new records must qualify in order to become official.

Since May 1972, Mr. Lighturn and I have organized tape-recorded interviews with himself and other outstanding Belizean athletes of years past. With the assistance of Radio Belize, these recordings are to be put into a biography of the history of Track and Field in Belize.

While working with Mr Lightburn to locate track and field records we found that the best performances set during the 1950s were below that of previous years. Two track meets were held in 1961 and 1962. No records were available from 1963 to 1970. Someone apparently screwed up. The markers I had surveyed and placed two years earlier made it possible to accurately mark the MCC Grounds. Bill and I don't know for how long people were guessing marked angles.

5.   EXPANSION OF THE ATHLETIC PROGRAM

The attached letter was sent to all secondary schools in the country, I have received positive replies from the following schools:

1. Muffles College
2. Fletcher College
3. Xavier College
4. Belmopan Comprehensive School
5. Austin High School
6. Wesley College
7. Junior Secondary School
8. St. John's College
9. Technical College

6.   TRAINING OF DORLA FLOWERS

In my second report I had mentioned that Dorla Flowers, a student from St. Hilda's College, had potential in the 100 meter and 200 meter races. At that time I felt that with proper training, she could qualify for the upcoming Olympic Games in Munich, Germany.

During last December, a program was started to develop this potential. By March it became evident that she did not have the self-motivation necessary to become an Olympic athlete and the program was terminated.

7.   COUNTERPART

When I wrote the previous report, I suggested the formation of a National Sports Council would be a desirable step towards uniform sports development in Belize. A sports Council could be organized similar in structure to the Tourists Board. The Ministry would provide a grant to pay the salary of a qualified director, who would function as the secretary of the Council. The council would be comprised of presidents from each sporting association, representative of the Ministry, Police, Volunteer Guard, and Army etc. Regular meetings would be held, and decisions of the Council carried out by the secretary (sports director).

On June 2, 1972, with the assistance of Ned Pitts, letters of inquiry were posted via the Ministry to nine Caribbean and Latin American countries. The letters asked for information on their National Sports Organizations. From replies to these letters and a further study of Belizean needs, a more thorough and comprehensive report shall be written with recommendations.

8.   PROPOSED PROJECTS

When one considers the value with which the Track and Field Clinics played this year in inspiring a nationwide participation in the sport, I would like to suggest the following projects beginning from this September. The request includes each district in the country.

1. Follow-up lectures on the training of athletes.
2. National Physical Performance Testing.

Follow up lectures would be open to any interested adult desiring to register. These advanced lectures would involve the techniques and theory of training athletes. One of the major objectives of this project is to create an awareness of the importance of proper and continued training.

The Physical Performance Testing would require co-operation from the secondary schools, since they would be the only way such a program would be successful.

As mentioned in the second report, physical performance testing is used to measure the physical standards of the nation's youth, to locate weaknesses and to create an awareness of the schools physical education effectiveness. The testing involves the student directly. Certificates of standard could be issued to those reaching a certain standard.

The testing measures the basic skill and strength related to all sports. This fact has much significance. Since the test shows the students' abilities as well as his weak areas, the compiled data of such testing will allow guided action to be taken by physical educators. Likewise, the testing along with certificates of achievement can encourage many of the boys and girls to want to develop their abilities, thus laying a better foundation for all sports in general.

Conducting the above mentioned projects would be a minimal expense to the Ministry: printing costs of certificates, my transportation costs and necessary stationary.

424

INDEX

A

Agriculture,
177,281,297,310
Agricultural Show, 83,
149,281-284,336
Aguilar, Raul, 68
Aguilar, Wilfredo, 359
Airport Camp,
60,68,125,126,147,
161,202,227,229,252,
255,367,394,
396,399,400
Albany, 17,441
Albert Academy, 5, 6
Albert Street, 56,70,
127,411
Albert, Dave PCV, 183,
186, 188
"Amazing Grace", 30
Ambergris Caye, 275,
276,278,341-343,
345,346,348
Amin, Idi, 99,172
Anabaptist, 196
Anderson, Dave, 51,
61,73,167,200,393,
394,396
Andrewin, Phylip, 233
Anglican, 80
Antigua, 151
Aralen, 15
Arana, Rudy, 111
Arawak Indians, 72
Ark Royal, 158

Archeology
Department, 183,188
Arguellas, Solie, 206
Atkins, Manfred,
338,339
Augustine, Dudley,
107, 108
Austin High School,
265,269,364,422
Authors, Minister,
368
Autotransportes de
Oriente, 239,271

B

Babb, Joan, 110
Badaya, 328
Bamboo, 10,191-193
Bamboo Bay
Nightclub, 66
Bamboo Clump, 208,
209
Bangura,
Allie, 22
Kekura, 21
Baron Bliss,
57,83,197,198,204-
210
Barranco, 101
Baymen, 144
Baymen Ave., 55,175
Belikan Beer, 127
Belisle, Mr., 320,335
Belizario, 161,163
Belize Defense Force,
229,396

Belize Estate and
Produce Company,
394
Belize Insurance Center,
396
Belize Jr. Secondary
School,
34,113,268,422
Belize Teachers' College,
111,192-195,277,418
Belize Technical
College, 264, 268
Belize
Telecommunication
Authority,
99,214,261-263,321
Belmopan
Comprehensive,
76, 212, 267, 268,
422
Belmopan, Miss, 296
Belizario, 161,163
Benjamin, I.E., 11
Bennett, Walter, 87, 88
Benque Nazarene, 374
Benque Roman,
Catholic, 374
Benque Viejo, 250
Bevis Ranch,
177,179-181
Bevis, Albert, 179,196
Big Falls, 179
Bird's Isle, 127
Bishop, Jane, 110
Blades, Lorraine, 110
Blanco, Teresita, 110

Bliss Institute, 57,
197,198, 204-206,
208, 209
Blue Creek, 158,189,
190
Bo Boxing Club, 15,22
Bo Rugby Club, 15
Bo School, 22,24
Bo School Band, 24
Bo Teacher Training
College, 6-8,26
Bofors, 159
Boledo, 64,65,67
Bonillo, Mauricia, 331
Bonthe, 16, 20
Bowing, Bruce, 385,
386
Brabaender, Susanne,
110
Bradley, Roy, 336,337
Brazil, 171
Brima, Prince, 19, 21,
24-26
British Broadcasting
Corporation, 18
British and
Commonwealth
Games, 138,153
British Foreign
Office, 44, 157
British Honduras
Amateur Athletic
Association, 87,105,
107,120,123,137

British Honduras Olympic Committee Association, 120,122,129

British Honduras Volunteer Guard, 153,229,249,250,391, 423

British West Indian Games, 137

Brooks, Huedney, 111

Brown, George, 110

Brown, Sylvia, 110

Buccaneer jets, 158

Bucknor Shipping Line, 344

Bud Benk Wedding, 205

Burdon Canal, 210

Bunce Island, 30

Burgess, Roy, 138

C

C.A.R.E, 178

Cabbinett, Eugene, 109

Cable and Wireless Company, 202

Cadenas Observation Post, 162,163

Cain, PCV Bill, 219, 220, 275

Cal, Raphael, 109

Calcium carbonate, 116

California, xxv,1,18,47, 93,196,239,241,243-245,398,401,404,441

Camp Holdfast, 161, 163,367,380

Canada, 49,153,196,271

Canoe, John, 295

Carballo, Ricardo, 110

Carcano, Winston, 227, 229

Carib, 72,178,320,325, 328,331

Caribbean Tobacco Company, 396

Cashew tree, 322

Cassava, 317,322, 324-332

Cassimirro, Alphonsa, 100

Castillo,
Joseph, 111
Othon, 110
Santiago, 68
Stanley, 111

Castro, George, 111

Catfish, 66

Catholic, 80,172,196, 343, 351, 374

Cattle Landing Camp, 161

Cattouse, Minister Albert, 90

Caucasian, 49

Cayo District, 36,161, 211,374,409

Cayo OP, 161,164

Cayo Primary School Athletic Association (CAPSAA), 367,374

Cave Branch, 186-188
Central American and Caribbean Games, 120, 123, 138
Central Farm, 35,367
Cernota, PCV Bill, 21
Cervantes,
  Francisco, 407,408
  Frank, 51,52,70,208,209, 282,313,405,407,411
Cessna A-37B Dragon Flies, 148
Chaffey College, 17,442
Chetumal, 137,239, 245, 246, 254
Chicken feed, 180-182
Chicle, 150
Chief Medical Officer, 178
Chinese, 49
Choithram's Super Market, 21
Cholera, 4, 18
Christ the King College, 16, 20
Christie, Anthony, 131
Church Street, 86
City of Industry, 244
Ciudad Melchor de Mencos, 161,164
Cobb, Benito, 110
Coconut tree, 322
Coleman
  Carl, 37,39,213, 391,409

Eddie Seferino, 58,59,323
Collet Canal, 53
Comal, 322,328
Commercial Center, 57
Commonwealth Games, 138, 153
Compton, Kelly, 32, 68, 219, 220
Conroy, Jerry, 52
Constanza, Solomon, 110,261
Conteh, K., 25
Continental, 68
Coronation Field, 24, 25
Corozal, 59,109,110,115, 127,132,137,179,239, 246,247,253,260,268, 269,351,418,419
Correa, Antonio, 110
Cox,
  Buck, 186-188
  Florence, 241
  Marilyn, 312
  Neil, 89
Coye, Richard, 131,137
Craig Street, 51,443
Creole, xxi,3,30,34,49, 54,59,62,96,127,178, 200, 239, 312,320,411
Cricket, 90
Cristo Ray, 374
Cruz, David, 109
Curran, Father, 23

D

Daily Mail, 27
Daily Report, 17
Daly Street, 85,420
DDT, 2
De La Haba, Louis, 83
Deeks. Gilda, 203
Deloes, Peter, 137
Dennison, Gilda, 110
Department of
  Agriculture, 183,188
Devil Dancer, 12,16,30
Devon and Dorset, 149,
  249,252,253,255,283
Dixon, PCV Chris, 119,
  211,374,376
Dominica, 151
Dominican Republic, 46
Donaldson, Eic, 72
Dream Book, 65
Duran, Mr., 333

E

Eagan, Percy, 116,117,
  119
East Africa, 18,191
East Canal, 53
East Indian, 49,172
Eastern Divisional
Track Meet,
115,121,133,134,360-
363
Eastern Illinois
  University, 17,257,277
Ecumenical Center, 77,
  80

Edith, Hurricane, 43,46
Ellen, Janis, 240,
  241,242,245,391
Ellis, Gilbert, 129
Emerald Isle Hotel, 276
Emma, 342
England, 31,44,55,90,
  124,147,151,152,
  157,158,254
Euphrates Ave., 200,
  410,411
Eva's Restaurant, 215
Evans, Fred, 122,123
Eve Street Canal, 54
Everitt, John, 72,150

F

F-51 Mustang, 148
Fairview Elementary
  School, 172,173
Fairweather Camp, 162
Fairweather, D.N.A.,
  249-251,256
Fairweather,
  Barbara, 33,203
  Betty, 203
  Norman, 72
  Sistie, 203,-
  205,210,249
  Terry, 204
Fandrei, Henry, 109
Fletcher College,
  115,260,269,353,354,
  358 359,422
Fletcher, PCV Frank, 7

429

Flores,
  Jacinto, 110
  Lydia, 111
Flowers,
  Dorla, 120,
  121, 138,417,422
  Franklin, 111,171
  Lennox, 293
  Lillette, 291,293
  William, 293
Forbes, C., 110
Ford, Nolan, 242,244
Fosbury Flop, 235
Four – 4-H,
  79,83,336,337
Franklin, Erasmo, 110
Frankson, Alex,
  31,32,41,73,93,
  275,411
Freetown Road, 68, 203,
  249, 251, 394
Freetown Rugby Club,
  18
Front Street Magistrate
  Building, 128
Fuller, Joseph, 129

G

Ganachos, 61
Garibaldi Plaza, 245
Garcia, Fred, 396
Garifuna, 49,72, 95-97,
  101,289,297,317
Gbundapi, 16
Gegg, Edgar, 110
Gentle, Rudy, 396

Ghana, 18
Gill, Eustace, 138
Gill, Lee, 79
Gillette, Morrell, 264
Gloucestershire, 1st
  Battalion, 146
Golden Bowl, 294
Gonzalez, Abigail, 100
Gonzalez, Alfredo, 110
Government Customs,
  60,275
Government Printers,
  72,271,273,309
Government Rest
  House, 213,320,321,
  325,373,375
Gracie Rock, 192,193
Grant, Inspector, 124
Grenada, 151
Grenadier Guards,
  124,125,127,128,140,
  147,157-159,228,231,
  233,234,236, 237,252
Gulliver, Major,
  124-126
Gurka, 166

H

Hall, Les, 155
Hammond, PCV Neal,
  46,175,180-182,270,
  391
Harrier Jets,
  160,161,165

Harris,
  Barbara, 33,203,251
  Francis, 251
  Lydia, 203,204, 251
  Neil, 203
Hattie, Hurricane, 47,
  75,101
Haulover Creek, 50,
  55, 57, 62, 63, 66,
  206-208
Hawkesworth Bridge,
  211,213, 375
Hecker, Francis, 111,
  171,172,333-335
Heyou, 328
Henderson, Edwin,
  110, 212
Hermans, Howard, 110
Hinkson, Gilmore, 67,
  124,128,131,152,227
  -229, 237, 286, 287,
  403-405
Hodgson, Sgt. Bill, 367,
  368,374,380,382
Holden Memorial
  Hospital, 34,311,411
Holy Angel Primary,
  370
Holdfast Camp,
  161,163,367,380
Holy Redeemer,
  61,313,407
Honduras,
  43,68,95,144,157,17
  9
Hong Kong, 72
Hopkins, 101,370

Houston United Athletic
  Club, 393-395
Hughes, Sgt. Allen, 229
Hummingbird Highway,
  98
Hurricane Edith, 43-46
Hattie, 47,75,101
Hyde,
  Evan X, 41
  Michael, 110,233
Hypolite, Douglas, 111

I
Ignacia, Sister, 333
India, 7,18,49,151,172
Inter-American
  Foundation, 181
International Farm
  Youth, 83
Irish Guard, 368, 381,
  382, 385, 390
Isabel, Hotel, Punta
  Gorda, 335
Isaacs, Leslie, 129
Islamic calendar, 12

J
Jackson, Ken, 11, 16, 20
Jaagus, PCV Tarmo, 175,
  405
Jamaica, 31,72,120,
  122,137,155,157,411
James, Sister, 262
Jehovah Witness, 172

Jones,
  Robert, 93
  Terrance, 91,311
Johnson, Randolph,
  396
Junior Secondary
  School,
  34,113,265,268,422

K

Keller, PCV Kent, 172
Kemp, Juanita, 103,
  107,131,140
Kennedy Club, 294
Kennedy,
  Joe, 5
  John, 175
  PCV Kim, 170
Kenyon-Bullard, Mary,
  73
King Street, 87
Kissy Town Road, 20
Kirk, Joyce, 110
Kolberg, PCV William,
  170,286
Kono Rugby Club, 18
Kramer,
  Sandra, 240,242
  Carole, 240
Krio, 3, 12, 34
Kroehl, Herb PCV, 91
Kulanda Town, 7

L

Ladyville, 71,210
LaUnión, 189,190

LaVerne College,
  1,17,142
Lawrence, Vin H.,
  72,273,308,309
Leacock, David CEO,
  272
Lebanese, 49
Leona, Sister, 107,262,
  263,352
Leppers, 21
Leslie, Rodwell, 111
Leslie, Roy, 411
Levy, Adrian, 109,212
Lewis,
  David, 111
  Ronald, 264
Lightburn, Bill, 67,87,
  90, 200, 285,313,338,
  390,409-414,421
Limba, 16
Lindsay, Oliver, 237
Lino, Francis, 110
Linn-Benton
  Community College,
  442
Lizarraga, Victor, 110
Locario, Bernadette,
  293
Logwood, 144,150
Lopez, Mr., 335
Los Angeles County
  Jail, 1,2
Lottery, 64,65
Lovell, Albert, 113-
  115,363,389
Lucas, Leroy, 138
Luna, Mayor, 211,212

Lungi International
    Airport, 29,30
Lynch, Father, 23

M

Macal River, 215
MacLeod, Barbara
    PCV, 183-188
Mahogany, 77,78,144-
    146,150,325,326
Mahuna, Anthony,
    111, 171
Makeni, 19
Malaria, 15
Malek, 309
Mangus, Teddy, 72
Marampa Mines, 18,23
Marin, Inair, 110
Marin, Mr. 61
Martinez,
    Alexandrina, 97,100,
    292,
    323,327,329,331
    Darius, 79, 95-98
    101,282,289,290,319
    ,332,336,370
    Gaynor, 289,290,293
    Luke, 111
    Domingo, 319
    Therese, 95
Marx, PCV Tad,
    405,407
Marylebone Cricket
    Club, 90
Maryski, Joe, 41
Masonic, 58
Mathews, Mr., 7

Maya Prince, 60
Mayan, 35,36,49,144,
    178,183-186,215, 249,
    253
Maypen, 178
McCarron, Mary, 110
Meighan, Norrin,
    128,129,136,228,374,
    375,409
Melchor de Mencos, 161
Melinda Road, 322,323
Memorial Park, 44,153
Mende, 12,30
Mendez, Javier, 109
Mennonite, 49,158,183,
    189,190,196,262
Mestizo, 49,178
Methodist, 80,172,260,
    370
Mexico, 138,145,152,
    157,158,181,189,196,
    235,239,240,245, 246,
    254,393
Michael,
    Eddie, 23
    Labib, 23
Michael's College, 268
Michigan, 79,313
Middleton, Evadne, 110
Ministry of Education,
    177, 259,272,418
Ministry of Health, 177-
    179
Miss Agriculture, 83,281
Mitchell, Robert,
    200,201,212,215,
    282,368,373

Monroe, Patsy, 202,203
Morey, Earl, 109
Moriano, Bob, 71,103, 107
Morris, E., 141,233
Mountain Pine Ridge, 35,166, 179,180
Mrs. Yorke's Infant School, 179
Muffles College, 107, 261,266,268,351, 352,422
Munich Olympic Games, 120,122,129,422
Muslim, 12,16

N

NAAFI, 126
Nash, Johnny, 72
National Agricultural Show, 83,149, 281-284,336
National Day, 43-45, 188
National Sports Council, 11,27,273,422
National Stadium, 64,284-287,314, 337,338
National Secondary School Track Meet, 131,132,137,139-141, 364,418,419
National Track and Field Course, 28,103,105, 109,171,417,418
National Youth Program, 72,273,308,310
Nazarene, 268,374
Nepalese, 166
Neal, Eric, 266
Netherlands, 196
New Orleans, 401,404
New Road, 68
Newton, John, 30
Nicaragua, 43,157
Nicol, N.K., 11
Nixon, Richard, xxvii, 175
Nolberto, Mayor Carlos, 135
Noralez,
Ann, 317,318
Martha, 326,331
Norman, Belizean driver, 32,411
North Atlantic, 158
North Front Street, 54, 56, 61-63,183,395
Northern Divisional Track Meet, 137,351-360
Northern Highway, 68, 69
Norway, 17
Nunez, Frank, 341,342,343, 348

O

O'Brien, Father John,
23
O'Connel, Major John,
128
Ochaeta, Hernan, 211,
368,369
Octathon, 123
Olympic,
29,120,122,129,138,
235,422
Ontario, 3,17,18,152,
239,242-244,404
Orange Walk, 59,107-
110,132,157,188,189,
219,253,261,262,266,
268,338,339,351-
359,418-420
Oregon State University,
273,277,279,398,403,
442
Oriole Street, 282

P

Pais, Francisca, 324,
331
Palace Theatre, 70
Palacio, Aloysius, 110
Palacio, Jorge, 128
Pallotti Convent, 45
Panama, 64,148
Panky, Steve, 212
Panning, Leon PCV, 172
Paulin, Sherwood
'Woody', 28

Pech, Hon. Guadalupe,
40
Pelayo, Jorge, 129
Perdomo, Lileth, 211
Perera, Steve, 233
Petroglyph Cave, 186-
188
Petterson, PCV Bob, 11,
23
Philadelphia, 5
Phlebotomist, 396
Phoenix Squadron, 150,
167
Physical Performance
Test, 257-259,
261,317,325,333,341,
344,424
Pickstock Street, 62,
183
Pickwick Club, 394,395
Pitt, Lois, 110
Pitts, Ned, 119,120,
122,129,132,138,364,
373,418
Plassey Camp, 161
Police Inspector Grant,
124
Police Special Forces
Unit, 70,71,73,107,
153, 227
Policelli
PCV Neil, 92,188,
190, 219-221
PCV Tony, 188-
190,219,220
Pomona, 1, 404
Poot, Fausto, 110

Portuguese, 172
Posnett, Governor
  Richard, 151-
  155,157,167,196,
  253,312
Posnett, Shirley, 233
Postal Inspector, 67,
  237
Powell, Richard, 110
Price Barracks, 161
Price, Honorable
  George,
  44,45,57,75,77,78,80,
  154,161,397,407
Prince Philip, 154
Public Market,
  57,63,200,247
Public Works
  Department,
  81,155,171,216,
Pueblo Viejo, 162
Puerto Modesto Mendez,
  162,163
Puerto Rico, 31,172
Pujehun, 17
Puma helicopter, 161,
  163
Punta Gorda, 59, 60,
  101,109,111,159,161,
  162,169,170-
  173,249,253,269,
  333-335,364,417,418

Q

Quan, Richard, 110
Queen's Birthday, 153

R

Radio Belize, 45,46,
  58,59,89,98,338,339,
  397,421
Ramadan, 12,14,16
Ramirez, Alfred, 111
Ramirez, Oscar, 294
Rapier anti aircraft
  missile, 160,161
Recinos, Josephine, 213
Regatta, 206-208
Regent Street West, 63,
  66,405
Reggae, 58,72
Reyes, Principal, 343
Rideau Camp, 162
Rivero, 401,403
Roacke, Miss, 138
Robb, Mary Jane, 79,
  83
Robinson Lodge,
  343,344,347
Roaring Creek, 373
Roe, Adrian, 396
Roe, Brian,
  393,395,396
Rose Garden, 68,69
Roman Catholic Primary
  School, 343
Romeo, Max, 72
Rosado, Phillip, 129
Royal Air Force, 159
Royal Artillery, 162
Royal Corps of
  Engineers, 159

Royal Corps of Signals, 159
Royal Mechanical Electrical Engineers (REME), 147
Rudge, Tony, 23
Rugby, Sierra Leone, 15,17,18,23
Freetown Club, 18
Kono Club, 18
SL Army, 18
Marampa Mines Club, 18
Rugby, Belize, 202,252,254,255,393, 396, 399,400,401

S

Sacred Heart, 370, 374
Saddleback Elementary, 172
Salamanca Camp, 162
Sales Si Puedes, 178
Salizar, Principal, 212
Sanchez, Jaime, 103, 107,411
Salvador, 68
San Carlo, 245,246
San Ignacio, 109,132, 161, 211-217,253, 267, 268, 367-369, 373-380,418,419
San Miguel, 253
San Pedro, 253,269, 275, 276, 341-348, 397

San Pedro Catholic Primary School, 343
San Antonio, Cayo, 374
San Antonio, Punta Gorda, 172
Sarita, Sister, 212
Santa Elena, 374
Sarstoon River, 162, 163
Schmidt, Harold, 110
Scots Guards, 147
Scotsman, 178
Sebiba, 325
Seferino, Eddie, 58, 59, 323
Seine Bight Village, 101
Seventh Day Adventist Primary School, 10
Sharp, PCV Rick, 52, 192,193,195, 254,255, 313,342-348,373- 375,405,406
Sherif, Ansumana, 14
Silva, Hector, 215,217
Simmons, Menno, 196
Sistie's Dance Troupe, 203-205,210,249
Skeen, William, 396
Slater, Dick, 126,127, 140,159,228
Smith,
Carl, 110
S.F., 138
Warren, 244
Smithford Products, 152,242-244

Snell Hall, Corvallis, 398

Social Development Department, 36-38,79,85,86,95,107, 108,126,137, 152,171,200,201,258, 260,277,282,308,310, 320,336,368,373

Southern Divisional Track Meet, 135, 136, 363

Southern Highway, 169, 170,186,334

Spanish, 31,49,59,144,198, 215,405

Spanish Lookout, 183

Speleologist, 183

St. Andrew's Primary, 211,374

St. Ann's Anglican Church, 80

St. Barnabas, 374

St. Catherine Primary School, 179

St. Francis, 374

St. Herman's Cave, 184

St. Hilda's College, 120, 121,422

St. John's College, 40, 198, 266, 268

St. Joseph Church, 183

St. Kitts, 151

St. Lucia, 151

St. Mary's Hall, 58

St. Matthew's Primary, 370

St. Peter Claver College, 269,333

St. Peter's College, 269, 276, 341,346

St. Vincent, 72

Stafford Youth Club, 34

Staging, 5

Staines, Enrique, 343,345,348 Elvi, 346

Stann Creek High School, 269,364

Stann Creek River, 291, 297, 298

Starner, Mark, 110

Stevens, Dr. Siaka P., 25, 26

Stewart, Shaun, 205

Studio Dansol, 206

Swayne, Sir Eric, 150

Swing Bridge, 55-57,67

Sylvestre, Hon. Louis, 36,37,91,339,344, 397,417

T

Taiama, Sierra Leone, 3, 4, 16,18

Teakettle, 159

Telecommunication tower, 99,214, 261-263, 321

Texas Instruments, 270

Thomas,
   Mr. & Mrs., 4,16,18
   Sigismond, 3
Thurston, Juanita, 411
Thurston, Rob, xxi-
   xxiii,33,41,170,171,
   390, 411
Tia River, 18
Tijuana, 152,239,240,
   245
Title 9,403
Toledo District,
   159,162-164
Toomey, Bll, 120
Torres, Edward, 109
Torwama, 26
Tosh, Peter, 72
Track and Field Course,
   103-107,109-
   111,115,117,219,246,
   333,417-419,420
Triangular Track Meet,
   123,126-
   129,134,139,227-
   229,231,381-390,420
Transporte del Norte,
   240, 245
Trophy King Awards,
   404
Tropical Storm Laura,
   97,98
Tucker, Mrs., 9

U
UBAD, 70
Uganda, 99,151,152,
   153,171,172
UNESCO, 191,196
United Nations Youth
   Advisor, 308
United States
   Consulate,
   31,43,45-47,70
Unitedville, 374
Unity Newspaper, 19

Usher,
   Chadwich, 388
   James,
   121,127,128,131,
   215,224,233
   Leni Jo, 40,198-
   200,215,411
   Michael, 129

V
Valentine, Jerris, 300,
   301,305
Vasquez, Nestor, 129
Vassel, Vernon, 103
Venice, 72
Victoria Street,
   51,62,407,408
Vietnam, 148
Vista Dance Studio, 210
Voice of America, 18

W

Waight,
  Eric, 387
  Michael, 109
  District Officer, 212
Wallace-Johnson, 27
Wanaragua, 295
Wangie River, 16
Warren, Don, 189,190
Washboard, 81
Weir, Danny, 66
Wesley College, 141
West Indies, 90,198
Western High School,
  212,267,268,380
Western Highway, 34,
  167
Wet marking box, 116,
  118,119
White, Rowland,
  150,159,167
Wilkinson Sword of
  Peace, 253,256
Wisconsin, 341
Witthohn, PCV Andy, 34
Woodfield, Lt. Bob,
  125,126,128,228
World Health
  Organization, 177
Wowla, 325,327
Wright, Mr., 334

X

Xavier College, 268,354
Xunantunich, 36, 215

Y

Yo Creek, 189,219-
  225,420
Yorke's Infant School,
  179
Young,
  Lloyd, 109
  Roy, 320
  Neville, 211

Z

Zetina, Jaime, 109
Zuniga, Jose, 211,213

The following works are used in this book under the Creative Commons Attribution-Share Alike 3.0 Unported License located at: http://creativecommons.org/licenses/by-sa/3.0/legalcode
The creators of these works do not endorse this book.

About the Author

Ted W. Cox was born in Eugene, Oregon, in 1947. He graduated from Chaffey Junior College, Southern California, in 1967. In 1969, he graduated from the University of La Verne (ULV), California, with a BA in physical education, and six years later from Oregon State University (OSU), Corvallis, Oregon, with an MS in education.

From 1969 to 1973, Cox served as a Peace Corps Volunteer in Africa and Central America. During 1975 and 1976, he taught physical education and first aid at Linn-Benton Community College (LBCC) in Albany, Oregon.

Since 1977, Ted has owned and operated the Old World Deli in downtown Corvallis. He has written three books: *When British Honduras Became Belize, 1971-1973; The Toledo Incident of 1925;* and *Murray Loop: Journey of an Oregon Family, 1808 – 1949.*

Also by Ted W. Cox

The Toledo Incident of 1925:
Three Days That Made History in
Toledo, Oregon
Available at www.oldworlddelipublications.com

Murray Loop: Journey of an
Oregon Family–1808 -1949
Available on Kindle